# AI ESSENTIALS FOR BEGINNERS

STEP-BY-STEP LESSONS, HANDS-ON ACTIVITIES, AND CUSTOM TOOLS TO LEARN & APPLY THE BASICS OF ARTIFICIAL INTELLIGENCE

ATWATER PUBLISHING

# CONTENTS

Introduction 7

1. DEMYSTIFYING AI 11
*Clarity Without Jargon*
1.1 Getting Comfortable with AI in Real Life 11
1.2 Machine Learning, Deep Learning, & Data Science 15
1.3 Narrow AI vs. General AI—Everyday Examples That Make It Click 17
1.4 Debunking the Top 5 Myths About AI 19
1.5 The AI Glossary—Your Visual Guide to Common Terms 22

2. AI IN YOUR DAILY LIFE 27
*Spotting the Invisible Helper*
2.1 AI at Home—From Smart Speakers to Streaming Recommendations 27
2.2 AI at Work—How AI Shapes Emails, Schedules, and Teamwork 30
2.3 AI on the Go—Navigation, Rideshares, and Smart Travel 32
2.4 AI in Healthcare—Virtual Doctors, Wearables, and Wellness 35
2.5 AI in Shopping—Personalized Ads, Recommendations, and Fraud Protection 38
2.6 Spotting AI—How to Tell If a Tool or Service Uses AI 41

3. HOW AI "THINKS" 43
*Step-by-Step Lessons with Visuals*
3.1 How AI Learns—The Recipe Analogy for Training Data 43
3.2 What's an Algorithm?—Simple Steps Behind Every AI Decision 46

3.3 Neural Networks as City Traffic—A Visual Walkthrough 49
3.4 Supervised vs. Unsupervised Learning—Sorting and Solving Puzzles 51
3.5 Testing a Free Image Recognition Tool 54
3.6 From Training to Inference—How AI Goes from Learning to Doing 56

4. HANDS-ON AI 61
*Practical, No-Code Exploration*
4.1 Talking to Chatbots—Conversational AI in Action 61
4.2 Exploring AI Art—Generating Images Without Coding 64
4.3 Voice Assistants—Customizing Alexa, Siri, and Google Assistant 67
4.4 Spotting Deepfakes—Hands-On with AI-Generated Media 70
4.5 Building a Personal AI Cheatsheet—Your Quick Reference Toolkit 73
4.6 Quick Quiz—Test Your AI Awareness with Everyday Scenarios 76

5. AI AT WORK 79
*Unlocking Everyday Productivity*
5.1 Automating Repetitive Tasks—AI Tools for Busy Professionals 79
5.2 AI for Teams—Collaborative Tools That Make Meetings Smarter 82
5.3 Using AI for Smarter Email and Calendar Management 88
5.4 AI in Customer Service—Chatbots and Beyond 91
5.5 AI in Hiring—Resume Screening and Bias Explained 94
5.6 Your AI Career Roadmap—Entry Paths for Non-Techies 97

6. ETHICS, BIAS, AND PRIVACY 99
*AI for Responsible Beginners*
6.1 Understanding AI Bias—Why It Happens and How to Spot It 99
6.2 Protecting Your Privacy—Safe AI Use at Home and Work 102
6.3 Black Box AI—Why Some Decisions Are Hard to Explain 105
6.4 AI and Fairness—Tackling Real-World Ethical Dilemmas 108
6.5 Evaluating AI News—Separating Hype from Reality 111
6.6 Instant Action—Simple Steps to Be an Ethical AI User 113

7. STAYING CURRENT 117
*Your AI Journey Beyond This Book*
7.1 The Hottest Trends—ChatGPT, Generative AI, and What's Next 117
7.2 AI News—Where to Find Reliable Updates 120
7.3 Curated Resources—Best Podcasts, Courses, and Websites for Beginners 122
7.4 Setting Up Your Personalized AI Learning Plan 125
7.5 Visual Glossary for Quick Reference 128
7.6 AI for Life—Applying What You've Learned to Everyday Decisions 129

Conclusion 133
References 137

# INTRODUCTION

Your phone pings with a new message. It's a birthday reminder, a weather alert, or maybe a friend's photo from last night's dinner. You didn't ask for any of it, but there it is—timely, precise, and almost uncanny in how well it fits your day. At the heart of this convenience is something most people rarely see: artificial intelligence. AI shows up in your social media feeds, your music playlists, and even your online shopping cart. It sits quietly behind the scenes, making recommendations, solving problems, and saving you time. Suddenly, AI feels everywhere—and it's not going away.

If you're like many people, you might feel a bit uneasy about it. Maybe you hear talk about AI at work and wonder if you're falling behind. You see headlines about robots taking jobs, smart assistants making decisions, or strange new tools that seem smarter than people. A voice in your head might say, "I'm not technical enough for this," or, "AI sounds complicated and scary." You are not alone. That sense of confusion and intimidation is real, and it's more common than you think.

Here's the truth: you don't need a computer science degree to use AI in your daily life. You don't have to be a math genius or even a tech enthusiast. What you do need is a clear, simple path. You need a resource that can show you how to use AI in ways that make sense for you—at work, at home, or wherever life takes you next.

This book is for people who want to learn about AI without feeling overwhelmed. If you've ever felt lost in a sea of jargon, you'll find straightforward explanations here. If you've wished for step-by-step lessons that build your confidence, you'll find them in every chapter. If you like to learn by doing, you'll discover practical exercises, visual guides, and real-life examples to help you put AI to work right away.

What makes this book different? Many books about AI start with deep theory or complex code. They talk about the rise of machines, deep learning algorithms, or the future of humanity. Instead, we focus on helping you use AI tools right now. You will learn how to write better emails, control privacy settings, organize your schedule, and spot fake news. You will see how AI can help with tasks big and small—without needing to know how it all works behind the scenes.

You will not find heavy math or dense technical language here. You will not need to memorize long lists of terms. Instead, you will find simple guides, checklists, and cheat-sheets that you can use whenever you need them. You will have a glossary to help you with common words and phrases you might encounter. You will find helpful visuals that explain even tricky concepts in clear steps.

The book is organized so you can start at the beginning or jump right to the topics that matter most to you. In the first chapters, you'll learn what AI is and how it fits into everyday life. Next, you'll get hands-on lessons for using popular AI tools. There are practice exercises to build your confidence, and "try it yourself" activities to help you remember what you've learned. At the end, you'll find cheatsheets and a glossary for quick reference whenever you need them.

Maybe you're thinking, "But I've never been good with computers." Or, "I'm too old to learn something new." Or perhaps, "I tried before and gave up." Many started with doubts, just like yours. With the right guidance, they discovered that AI was not only approachable but also enjoyable. You do not have to be perfect. You only need to start, and we will help you every step of the way.

This book is not just something to read. It's something to use. Some chapters will ask you to try exercises or answer questions. Others will challenge you to use what you've learned in your own life. The more you participate, the more you'll gain. If you skip the exercises, you might still learn something. But if you take part, you will build real skills, real confidence, and real understanding.

You might feel nervous about starting. That's natural. But you hold in your hands a guide designed just for you. Our goal is to help you move from confusion to confidence. From hesitation to action. From wondering about AI to using it in ways that help you every day.

AI is not just for tech experts. It's for everyone. Let's take the first step together.

# CHAPTER 1
# DEMYSTIFYING AI
## CLARITY WITHOUT JARGON

Ever noticed how your email filters out junk like lottery scams and sales pitches and moves them straight into the Spam folder? Or how your phone gives you the weather the moment you ask, no typing required? These everyday conveniences are made possible by artificial intelligence (AI). While it may seem mysterious and overly technical, AI is simply a part of daily life, quietly making things easier and smarter.

## 1.1 GETTING COMFORTABLE WITH AI IN REAL LIFE

You don't need to overhaul your entire routine to start seeing how AI is already woven into your daily habits. The reality is, AI blends into the background, quietly enhancing the way you work, learn, and even relax. Consider how you interact with apps on your phone or computer. When you search for a file by typing just a few letters and it pops up instantly, there's a good chance AI played a part. These systems learn from your previous searches, picking up on patterns and becoming more accurate over time. Have you ever wondered how your favorite photos automatically get sorted into albums or how those "memories" videos show up without any effort from you? That's AI, sorting and selecting in the blink of an eye.

The workplace has shifted, too. Think about those calendar invites that practically schedule themselves or the meeting notes that appear in your inbox after a call. Many companies use AI-powered transcription tools that transform spoken words into searchable text, making it easy for you to recall what was said or share key points with colleagues who couldn't attend. Even customer service has changed: instead of waiting on hold forever, you might interact with a smart system that can answer basic questions, route you to the right person, or even help reset your password—saving everyone time.

Education is another area where AI makes an impact without drawing attention. Online learning platforms use AI to personalize lessons and quizzes, adapting the material based on what you get right or wrong. It's like having a tutor who knows just where you need help and which topics you've already mastered. Some schools and universities now use AI to flag potential plagiarism or to recommend extra reading materials tailored to your interests.

AI-driven creativity tools are everywhere, helping people brainstorm ideas, write stories, or even compose music without needing years of training. It might sound odd to mix "AI" and "creativity," but these tools can suggest catchy headlines, generate artwork from simple sketches, or remix songs based on your mood. These aren't just for artists or designers —anyone can try them and see instant results.

Of course, convenience is only part of the story. There's a growing emphasis on using AI responsibly—especially when it comes to privacy. Your devices often give you control over what data gets used for improving services. It's wise to check your settings now and then, especially if you're using a new app or smart device. Most companies offer clear options for opting in or out of data collection, and some even let you see what information has been gathered. Staying aware of these choices helps you enjoy the benefits of AI while keeping your comfort and privacy in mind.

Another important aspect is accessibility. AI has opened doors for many people who once faced barriers due to disabilities or other challenges. Speech-to-text converters help those who struggle with typing; text-to-speech readers make online content available to people with vision impairments; translation tools break down language walls in seconds. These technologies aren't just for tech gurus—they're designed for anyone who wants to make life a little easier.

It's easy to feel overwhelmed by the flood of buzzwords and headlines about AI breakthroughs. But when you break it down, most of what matters comes back to small, practical improvements—tiny tweaks that add up over time.

***Reflection: Where Do You Notice AI?***

Pause for a second and think about where AI might be supporting you right now, even if you didn't notice it before. Is it recommending recipes based on what's in your fridge? Reminding you of bills that are due? Translating a news article from another language? Make a list of three moments from today or this week when technology made something smoother, faster, or more enjoyable. You might be surprised by just how often these tools are helping behind the scenes.

Looking ahead, try to approach new technologies with curiosity rather than apprehension. The next time an app prompts you with a suggestion or an automated tool offers help, take a closer look: What's actually happening? Is there an opportunity to save time or learn something new? AI isn't here to replace what makes us human—it's here to give us more space for creativity, connection, and growth.

As we move forward, keep an open mind and remember that every skill—no matter how advanced it sounds—starts with small steps and simple understanding. The more familiar you become with these tools, the more empowered and confident you'll feel, not just as a user of technology but as someone who can shape how it fits into your own life.

## 1.2 MACHINE LEARNING, DEEP LEARNING, & DATA SCIENCE

If all the buzzwords—machine learning, deep learning, data science, and artificial intelligence—feel confusing, you're not alone. These terms are often used interchangeably, but each has clear distinctions.

A helpful way to picture the structure of AI is to imagine a set of Russian nesting dolls. The largest, outermost doll represents **artificial intelligence (AI)**—the broadest concept. AI includes any system designed to imitate human thinking or problem-solving, whether it's a chess program or a conversational chatbot. It serves as the overarching layer that encompasses all the others.

The next layer within the structure is **machine learning**. In this stage, computers move beyond simply following fixed instructions—they learn from examples. Think of it like training a dog to shake hands: with repetition and positive reinforcement, the dog gradually understands what's expected. Similarly, in machine learning, computers analyze large amounts of data—such as thousands of pet photos—to recognize patterns. They don't memorize each image; instead, they learn to generalize from the examples they've seen.

Tucked within machine learning is **deep learning**. Deep learning uses digital "brains" called neural networks, loosely inspired by the human brain's structure. These networks are made up of multiple layers—each passing its input to the next, building up a collective understanding. This technique enables complex tasks such as recognizing faces, translating languages, and interpreting speech. If your phone recognizes your face or your voice assistant understands you over background noise, deep learning is likely behind it.

Where does **data science** fit in? Data science is a related but distinct field that focuses on collecting, cleaning, analyzing, and interpreting data to extract insights or support informed decisions. Think of data scientists as detectives hunting for hidden clues in data. While they might use AI or machine learning tools, they often rely on statistics and charts alone—such as determining which products sell best at a store—without necessarily utilizing AI.

These areas often overlap, which can make things confusing, but the differences still matter. A data scientist isn't always working with AI—sometimes they're simply analyzing sales numbers or customer trends. Not every machine learning project uses deep learning either; simpler tasks like sorting emails or suggesting products don't need it. And not every AI system depends on machine learning—some still run on straightforward, rule-based programs.

Do you use a favorite music app? You've probably noticed how it recommends songs you might like. That recommendation system is powered by **AI**. The part that figures out your personal taste based on what you listen to is **machine learning**. And if the app can recognize your voice in a noisy room or identify a song from just a short clip, that's **deep learning** at work. Behind the scenes, **data scientists** look at the big picture. They study listening habits and trends—like which genres are becoming popular in different cities—to help guide smarter business decisions.

If you're ever tangled up in terminology, remember the Russian nesting dolls: AI is the largest doll, machine learning sits inside, deep learning is inside that, and data science is a partner nearby—focused on making sense of data, with or without AI.

## 1.3 NARROW AI VS. GENERAL AI—EVERYDAY EXAMPLES THAT MAKE IT CLICK

Picture this: you open Google Maps, because you're running late in heavy traffic. The app checks road conditions, construction, and car flow, quickly suggesting a detour that saves you time. This isn't magic—it's narrow AI in action.

Narrow AI is built for a specific problem. It doesn't handle unrelated tasks like making dinner suggestions or answering your emails. Think of Spotify (a music app) making a playlist tailored to your mood or your phone predicting your next word. The AI focuses only on its goal, whether that's recommending songs or completing sentences, by learning from your habits and usage patterns. That's it. It doesn't branch out into unrelated skills.

Narrow AI is everywhere and usually blends into the background. Website chatbots handle shipping or return questions, but if you ask them about Paris weather or last night's game, they're lost. Autocomplete predicts your text because it's learned from millions of conversations. Your bank's fraud detector watches for unusual spending but won't advise on investments or your exercise routine.

This specialization is narrow AI's strength and its limitation. Every current example is built on processing specific data, applying learned patterns, and producing results within those rules. It cannot improvise or cross over to unrelated areas. Try to make Google Maps write your grocery list, and you'll get nowhere.

Now think about how movies and science fiction portray AI. They often imagine a kind of general intelligence that can handle any mental task like solving problems, telling jokes, creating art, repairing machines, or offering career advice. This type of AI would be able to learn new things on its own, move easily between different tasks, understand emotions, and work with abstract ideas, all without being programmed for each specific job. It would represent a broad and flexible form of intelligence.

But in reality, general AI doesn't exist. Everything we use today is narrow AI. No chatbot can drive a car. No navigation app can debate philosophy. No voice assistant can play chess unless separately programmed. The gap between today's systems and sci-fi AI is vast and experts believe we're decades away from reaching true general AI.

Media and entertainment often blur this line, suggesting that "AI will take over everything"—but they're referencing a fantasy type of general AI. For practical purposes, you don't have to worry about your tools suddenly gaining intent or independence. They just aren't designed that way.

Many people feel uneasy when they hear stories about machines becoming "too smart" or taking over jobs. The truth is that narrow AI surpasses humans only in repetitive or data-intensive tasks within a specific area. These include things like scanning resumes for keywords or examining medical images. However, it cannot replicate human intuition, creativity, or the ability to make wide-ranging decisions. It does not set its own goals or act beyond the rules it was programmed to follow. Even the most advanced chatbots that handle customer service still operate within clearly defined limits.

Narrow AI's real strength lies in automating clear, repetitive tasks, allowing people to focus on more meaningful work. It's not an all-powerful overlord or a self-aware system—it's simply a practical tool designed to make certain jobs easier.

Consider a workplace handling dozens of customer requests daily. A chatbot answers basic questions like store hours, order tracking, and password resets. This frees up employees for complex, human-centric tasks requiring empathy or creative problem-solving. Customers get fast answers to simple questions, and staff dedicate their energy to building relationships and handling unique issues.

So, whether you're using AI for route planning or to finish a text, you're collaborating with narrow AI. Its capabilities are focused and reliable; it's here to assist, not replace you. All the tools and examples discussed in this book rely on narrow AI for practical, real-world solutions for today. General AI remains a distant concept, not something you need to worry about now.

## 1.4 DEBUNKING THE TOP 5 MYTHS ABOUT AI

You might be surprised how many tall tales and wild stories swirl around artificial intelligence. These myths pop up at family dinners, in the news, and sometimes even in workplace meetings. You've probably lost count of how many times you have heard someone claim, "AI will take everyone's job," or "Pretty soon, machines will think for us." Let's set the record straight—together, we'll chip away at the biggest misconceptions so you can spot them a mile away.

**Myth one: "AI can think and feel like a human."**

This idea gets a lot of attention, especially with movies depicting robots falling in love or plotting world domination. The truth is, AI can't think, feel, or have opinions. It doesn't get nervous before a big presentation or excited about a promotion. It works by analyzing patterns in information—nothing more. A great example is when your voice assistant completely misunderstands a simple request. Have you ever asked your smart speaker to play a song, only for it to call someone instead? That's not an emotional meltdown; it's a data hiccup. The machine doesn't "know" anything in the human sense. It simply matches what you say to its training data and sometimes gets it wrong. If AI truly felt, it might apologize or send you flowers after a mistake, but as it stands, you get a robotic "Sorry, I didn't understand that."

**Myth two: "AI will soon take everyone's job."**

This one causes anxiety and pops up whenever technology changes how things are done. While some jobs may shift or change, history shows that new tools typically create new roles rather than simply eliminating old ones. Think about how ATMs changed banking—tellers still work in banks, but now help customers with more complex needs instead of just handling cash. AI can sort through large piles of paperwork or spot trends in sales figures faster than any person, but it can't replace the wit of a teacher or the hands-on care of a nurse. Even in offices using AI to sort resumes, real people make the final hiring decisions and ask the interview questions.

**Myth three: "AI is always right and unbiased."**

This particular myth gets people into trouble. AI is only as good as the data and instructions behind it. If the information it learns from is flawed or skewed, its results will be too. For instance, if an AI is trained on photos that mostly feature one group of people, it might struggle to recognize faces outside that group. Sometimes, an autocorrect tool changes your words into something embarrassing or confusing because it can't read your mind or know your intent.

**Myth four: "AI is only for techies or programmers."**

This assumption keeps many people from even trying out new tools. The reality? You use AI every time you unlock your phone with your face or get directions on your GPS. You don't need to write code or build robots to benefit from AI. Many no-code tools let you automate tasks or create smart routines with a few clicks or taps.

**Myth five: "AI is just a fad and will soon disappear."**

This one comes from a place of skepticism, which is understandable given all the hype. But AI isn't a passing trend like fidget spinners or viral dances. It continues to evolve and blend into more aspects of daily life, including healthcare, entertainment, shopping, communication, and even cooking.

Sure, some buzzwords come and go, but the ability to use smart tools for everyday tasks is here to stay.

Remember: when something about AI sounds too good (or too scary) to be true, it's worth questioning—and now you have the tools to do just that.

## 1.5 THE AI GLOSSARY—YOUR VISUAL GUIDE TO COMMON TERMS

AI buzzwords have a way of showing up everywhere—articles, workplace memos, even small talk at the coffee machine. Maybe you've seen terms like "algorithm," "prompt," or "neural network" and wondered if you should nod along or Google it later. That's exactly why this visual glossary exists. It's a quick-reference guide, whether you're reading at your desk, the kitchen table, or on the bus. Each word comes with a one-sentence definition and a down-to-earth comparison. You'll spot themes—grouped for when you need to quickly scan terms used in daily life, how AI "learns," or when talk turns to ethics and bias.

### 🔍 Core AI Concepts Explained in Everyday Terms

- **Algorithm**
  - An algorithm is a set of rules or instructions that AI follows to solve a problem or make a decision.
  - Think of a cake recipe: step-by-step instructions that lead to a desired result.
- **Training Data**
  - Training data is the information AI uses to learn patterns, recognize faces, or spot trends—it's

  what the system practices with to improve over time.
  - Imagine a family photo album that teaches relatives who's who.
- **Neural Network**
  - The "roads" carry bits of information, and the "intersections" (nodes) help AI analyze complex tasks.
  - Picture a city map filled with roads and intersections.
- **Prompt**
  - In AI, a prompt is the question or instruction you give to trigger a response.
  - It's like asking a friend for advice or directions—you provide context, and they respond.
- **Inference**
  - This is the AI's process of drawing conclusions from what it has learned.
  - It's similar to how a detective pieces together clues to make an educated guess.
- **Model**
  - This is what AI uses to make decisions after learning from data.
  - The trained "brain" of an AI system.
- **Output**
  - The response or result you see after giving the AI input (like a voice command to an assistant).
  - Example: The assistant listens (input), processes with its model, then responds (output).

## ⚖️ Ethics & Fairness in AI

- **Bias**
  - In AI, bias occurs when training data is unbalanced or when the algorithm learns unfair patterns, resulting in skewed or discriminatory outcomes.
  - It's like always listening to the same music playlist until the app assumes that's the only kind of music you like.
- **Transparency**
  - Transparency in AI means being able to see and understand how decisions are made.
  - It's like being able to read nutrition labels on food.

## 🔧 Common Technical Terms Made Simple

- **API (Application Programming Interface)**
  - A bridge that allows different programs to communicate
  - It's like two departments using a shared walkie-talkie channel.
- **Dataset**
  - A collection of organized data.
  - Think of it like combining all your music playlists into one giant library.
- **Reinforcement Learning**
  - Learning through trial and error with rewards
  - It's similar to training a pet with treats for good behavior.

- **Generative AI**
  - Tools that can create new content based on patterns they've learned.
  - Like text, artwork, or music.

To help make these stick, here's how we suggest using this glossary: mark or flag these pages so you can jump back anytime these terms pop up. If you see a word in an article or tool that feels intimidating, check here first before opening yet another search tab. You might even keep a sticky note handy for new terms you spot elsewhere.

Don't let jargon slow you down. This glossary is yours to revisit anytime—no shame in flipping back as often as you need. You're building real fluency every time you pause to check or clarify. The more familiar these words become, the more confident and capable you'll feel navigating conversations about AI in any setting.

---

***Quick Exercise: Jargon Spotting***

Grab a pen and highlight three words in this chapter that were new to you. Write them in your notebook with their analogies beside them. Next time those words pop up in conversation or online, you'll feel ready instead of lost.

---

# CHAPTER 2
# AI IN YOUR DAILY LIFE
## SPOTTING THE INVISIBLE HELPER

## 2.1 AI AT HOME—FROM SMART SPEAKERS TO STREAMING RECOMMENDATIONS

It's amazing how much technology has quietly made its way into our homes—often without us even noticing. You might wake up, still groggy, and your smart speaker is already one step ahead of you. Maybe you say, "Hey Google, what's the weather?" or "Alexa, play my morning playlist." There's no magic behind it—just AI recognizing your voice and learning from your daily habits. If you usually ask for the news right after your alarm, it soon starts offering it automatically, saving you a few extra steps and making your morning routine smoother. It's like having a personal assistant who remembers you like jazz on Wednesdays and a traffic report before heading out the door.

The way AI adapts is both subtle and impressive. Over time, your smart speaker notices if you skip certain songs or ask for different genres depending on the day. Suppose you never finish a podcast episode in the morning, but listen to it all the way through on weekends. In that case, AI will remember that and suggest longer shows on Saturdays. The more you use it, the better it gets at predicting your needs, quietly weaving itself into your daily habits. You don't have to do anything special—just live your life, and AI tunes in.

Ever wonder why Netflix always seems to know what you'll binge next? It's not just luck. Netflix's recommendation engine takes note every time you watch, pause, rewind, or abandon a show halfway through. The system learns about your tastes—maybe it picks up on your love for quirky comedies or dark thrillers. If you skip over romance movies but never miss a true crime documentary, Netflix's AI adjusts its suggestions, bringing more of what you crave to the front page. According to recent reports, about three-quarters of what folks watch on Netflix comes straight from these personalized picks.

The same idea powers Spotify and other music apps. Next time you notice a playlist pop up that seems tailor-made for your mood—maybe "Chill Sunday Vibes" or "Workout Hits" —know that AI tracked not just which songs you played but when, how often, and whether you skipped them. If you keep replaying certain tracks, Spotify's algorithm responds by surfacing similar artists or tunes with that same energy. This personalization doesn't just save time; it often introduces you to new favorites before you even know what you're looking for.

AI isn't limited to entertainment or music; it has quietly reshaped how homes run, too. Think about smart thermostats that learn when you're home and when you're out.

Set your preferences a few times, and soon it'll heat up the living room before you get back from work and cool things down just as you go to sleep. It watches patterns: if every Wednesday everyone leaves by 8 a.m., it dials back the energy use. Over time, these adjustments save money and make life more comfortable without constant fiddling.

Security at home has also leveled up thanks to AI. Modern security cameras don't just record—they recognize familiar faces or even pets. Instead of alerting you every time a squirrel runs past the door, smart cameras use AI to tell the difference between people, animals, or even vehicles. Some systems can even send a ping when your dog is at the back door or let you know if someone unfamiliar approaches. This helps cut down on false alarms and adds real peace of mind.

---

***Try This: Spot Your AI Sidekick***

Pick one device in your home—a smart speaker or streaming service is perfect. Ask Alexa for today's weather, or check which shows Netflix has lined up "Just For You." Next, think about why these suggestions appeared. Did Netflix recommend a new season of a show you watched last year? Did your music app shuffle in songs from an artist you recently liked? Write down three ways you notice AI helping (or surprising) you this week.

---

## 2.2 AI AT WORK—HOW AI SHAPES EMAILS, SCHEDULES, AND TEAMWORK

There's a quiet revolution happening behind your computer screen, and it's all about making work feel less like a grind and more like a flow. If you've ever looked at your inbox and wondered how all those scam emails get filtered out, you've already seen AI working for you. Spam filters are no ordinary gatekeepers—they use algorithms that scan for patterns, dodgy keywords, and odd sender addresses. Over time, these systems notice what you always send to trash and what you open first. That means your priority inbox learns who matters to you, shuffling boss emails up top and hiding the endless subscription noise. It's as if your email finally started reading your mind, sorting messages before you even wake up.

Meetings, often the headache of office life, become easier to manage with AI tools. Smart scheduling assistants review calendars, find open slots, and propose times that work for everyone. Instead of endless email chains asking, "How about Tuesday at 2?" the system checks availability automatically and even follows up with people who haven't responded. Over time, these tools learn your preferences—whether you like morning check-ins or prefer to keep lunch open—and quietly protect your schedule. They help you avoid double-bookings and save you from those draining, late-day meetings when your focus is gone.

Communication platforms like Slack and Microsoft Teams have introduced new AI features that transform scattered chats into something actually useful. Say you're on a video call with teammates across three time zones and someone starts speaking in a language you don't quite catch. Real-time translation works to turning fast French or rapid Spanish into clear English subtitles as the speaker talks. This isn't science fiction. It's built right into modern workplace tools. Even background noise gets filtered out by AI, so barking dogs or coffee shop chatter fade into silence during meetings.

You've probably noticed chatbots popping up in coporate channels, too. These aren't just for customer support anymore; they help with everyday tasks like answering HR questions or guiding new employees through onboarding. Maybe you've clicked on one that explained how to reset your password or pointed you to the correct benefits form. These bots get smarter every week by learning from the questions people ask most often and tweaking their answers for clarity. It frees up human colleagues to focus on bigger challenges instead of answering "What's the Wi-Fi password?" for the hundredth time.

---

***Want to See This in Action?***

Here's a quick experiment: open up Gmail and look at a message in your inbox. Have you noticed the little Smart Reply buttons? These are short responses AI has generated based on the email's content. Try clicking one; it saves you time and helps with writer's block when all you need is a quick "Thanks!" or "Let's do it." If you manage calendars for yourself or your team, schedule a meeting using the assistant in Google Calendar or Outlook and watch how suggested times pop up as soon as you add invitees.

Platforms like Microsoft Teams offer another taste of what's possible. During your next virtual meeting, turn on the noise suppression setting and pay attention to how it blocks background distractions without cutting out your voice. You can experiment with live captions or translation features too. They're surprisingly accurate and help everyone follow along.

---

## 2.3 AI ON THE GO—NAVIGATION, RIDESHARES, AND SMART TRAVEL

You might not notice it, but every time you leave your house and reach for your phone to figure out where you're headed or how to get there, AI is working behind the scenes. Take navigation apps like Google Maps or Waze. These tools quietly gather data from thousands—sometimes millions—of phones moving around a city. They don't just show a static map. Instead, they analyze traffic speeds, delays, and even road closures in real time. If an accident pops up ahead or a new construction site slows traffic, then your map instantly adjusts your route to shave minutes off your trip. This isn't just about finding the shortest distance; it's about predicting what will actually happen on the roads by the time you get there. When your app says, "Traffic is heavy, but you're still on the fastest route," that's AI sorting through mountains of information, using algorithms to estimate how long you'll be stuck, and recalculating if a faster path opens up.

It's wild to think how much smoother travel has gotten with these tools. Remember when you had to check printed directions or ask someone at the gas station? Now, it's normal for your phone to buzz with a "time to leave" reminder or a heads-up about unexpected slowdowns. Predictive alerts aren't guesses. They come from AI looking at patterns from previous days, special events, and even weather reports.

Open up a ridesharing app like Uber or Lyft, and you'll see another layer of behind-the-scenes intelligence at work. When you request a ride, the system doesn't just send the nearest driver. It weighs factors such as distance, traffic, driver ratings, and the likelihood that a driver will accept before making a match. In seconds, it connects you with someone who can reach you quickly and efficiently. Ever notice how prices seem to jump during rush hour or when it's raining? That's dynamic pricing—AI watching demand spike in real time and adjusting fares so drivers have more incentive to hit the road. It's not always fun for your wallet, but it does mean you're more likely to get a ride when everyone else wants one too.

Many city transit systems now rely on AI-powered tracking to predict bus and train arrivals with impressive accuracy. These systems pull in streams of data—from GPS sensors on vehicles, traffic patterns on the roads, and even historical route performance—to calculate when the next bus or train will actually show up. If your ride is delayed, the app doesn't just leave you guessing. It provides an estimated arrival time that refreshes every few seconds as conditions change across town. This real-time insight helps riders plan better, whether that means grabbing a coffee while you wait or deciding to take a different route altogether.

Planning longer trips brings even more AI into play. Travel websites and apps use chatbots to help book flights, recommend hotels, or suggest local attractions based on what you like. Maybe you mention "family-friendly" or "pet-friendly" in a search—the AI behind the scenes scans reviews and listings to pull out options that match those words. Some chatbots even remember your preferences from past trips. If you loved a particular type of hotel last time, don't be surprised if similar places pop up next time you plan a getaway.

It's not just about booking hotels or flights, either. Many apps now suggest things to do based on your travel history or interests. Some AI systems even check opening hours and weather forecasts before making recommendations, so that your plans aren't spoiled by rain or surprise closures.

---

***Try This: Notice the AI on Your Next Trip***

The next time you're heading somewhere—whether it's across town or across the country—pick one travel-related app to use along the way. If you're requesting a ride, pay attention to how long it takes for a driver to be assigned and whether the price changes before you confirm. See if your route updates mid-trip due to unexpected traffic or roadwork. If you're using public transit, check how often your arrival times update as buses or trains move through their stops. For those planning a vacation online, note any personalized suggestions from chatbots or booking tools. Do they feel uncannily accurate? Jot down a few examples of how these apps adapt in real time based on what's happening around you.

---

Every small update inside an app, like changing a driving route, adjusting prices, or suggesting something new at the last minute, comes from AI sorting through loads of data to make your trip easier and less stressful. It is easy to forget how much guesswork these features have quietly taken out of getting around or planning your next adventure.

## 2.4 AI IN HEALTHCARE—VIRTUAL DOCTORS, WEARABLES, AND WELLNESS

You might not realize it, but your health has probably already been touched by AI. Take smartwatches and fitness trackers for example. These devices are strapped to wrists all over your office, gym, or family gatherings. They do much more than count steps. These wearables track your heart rate, monitor your sleep patterns, and even check how well you recover after exercise. The sensors inside collect streams of data like every heartbeat, restless toss in bed, or brisk walk around the block. AI sorts through this maze, looking for patterns and nudging you with reminders to stand up or warning you when your heart rate spikes unexpectedly. Instead of guessing how much sleep you got, you see your actual sleep cycle divided into light, deep, and REM phases. Some trackers even spot irregular rhythms that could signal bigger issues, pushing you to check in with a doctor before a small problem becomes worse.

Additionally, AI supports wellness by helping people take charge of their everyday health. Telemedicine has become a lifeline for busy people, parents juggling work and kids, or anyone living far from a clinic. Scheduling a virtual appointment can be as easy as tapping an app. AI-powered chatbots now handle first-line questions before you even see a human doctor. Imagine getting a sore throat late at night. You open an app, answer a few questions about your symptoms, and the AI sorts through your responses to suggest whether you should rest, seek medical advice soon, or head to urgent care now. These virtual helpers use natural language processing, which means they actually "understand" what you type, not just keywords.

Virtual doctors and AI-driven apps are also changing how people interact with healthcare providers. You don't always need to wait for office hours or sit in crowded waiting rooms. Instead, AI can review your history and symptoms, sometimes even flagging trends over weeks or months that you might miss. For example, someone tracking their blood sugar with a connected device could get instant feedback on how meals or exercise affect their numbers, making it easier to spot what helps or hurts their progress. All this data gets stored securely (with privacy built in), so it's easy to share with a real doctor during checkups.

Medication reminders are another place where AI shines. If you've ever forgotten to take your pills (or worried about a loved one who does) there are apps that learn your habits and ping you at just the right time. They adjust if you snooze or skip a dose, so the reminders come when you're most likely to act on them. Some even check in with gentle encouragement if days go by without a response. It's oddly reassuring to know there's an extra layer of support keeping tabs on something so vital.

Prevention is where AI starts to feel like a real safety net instead of just a convenience. Imagine a wearable that doesn't just track steps but detects heart rhythms that seem off. If your device notices something like atrial fibrillation (a kind of irregular heartbeat that can lead to stroke) it can send an alert straight to your phone. Early warnings like these allow people to catch problems before they become serious. Some smartwatches monitor oxygen levels or stress signals. Others can even detect falls and automatically call for help if you don't respond within a set window. These features have a real impact on seniors or anyone managing chronic conditions.

As an example, here is a scenario that's becoming more common. Picture someone who never paid much attention to their heart rate until their watch buzzed with an alert one afternoon. The device had noticed an irregular pattern—nothing dramatic, just enough of an outlier compared to their usual readings. At first, they shrug it off, but the alert persisted over several days, and it prompts them to book an online appointment with a doctor who reviewed not just the symptoms but also the watch's recorded data. The result? They were sent for further tests and discovered a minor issue before it could become a crisis.

## 2.5 AI IN SHOPPING—PERSONALIZED ADS, RECOMMENDATIONS, AND FRAUD PROTECTION

Have you ever noticed how online shops seem to know exactly what you want, sometimes before you do? That's not magic. It's AI, quietly taking notes on what you browse, what sits in your cart, and even which items you click on but ignore. Open an app like Amazon or your favorite grocery site and see a carousel of suggested products. Most of them are based on what you've looked at recently, what similar shoppers bought, or even what you grabbed last week. Maybe you searched for running shoes yesterday and now see a pop-up for moisture-wicking socks or a deal on fitness trackers. The system isn't just guessing; it's analyzing patterns in your actions, and sometimes those suggestions are so spot-on it almost feels spooky.

Personalized email offers work the same way. You sign up for a newsletter, and suddenly your inbox fills with deals tailored to your style, size, or favorite colors. If you often buy coffee pods every few weeks, don't be shocked when a coupon appears right before you'd usually run out. Grocery apps might nudge you with reminders about your regular staples or suggest recipes based on the items in your cart. All this happens because AI studies your habits and nudges you toward things it thinks will catch your eye. Sometimes these nudges are helpful and other times it can feel overwhelming. The trick is to recognize when AI is lending a hand and when it's just trying to nudge you into another purchase.

Targeted advertising takes this a step further. AI doesn't just see what you buy, it also tracks things like how long you linger on a product page, which reviews you read, and whether you compare prices before making a choice. If you look at camping gear on one site, don't be surprised if tents and sleeping bags start appearing in ads on your social media or while reading the news. That's because AI-powered ad networks share data across sites, building a profile of your interests. This helps companies show you products they think fit your taste or needs. For many people, this feels both convenient and a bit unsettling—after all, who wants to feel like their every click is being watched? But it's all part of how modern online shopping works. Your browsing history predicts what you might want next.

At the same time, there's a powerful upside: fraud protection. Credit card companies and payment services rely on AI to scan for odd patterns that could mean trouble. Ever get a call or text about a "suspicious transaction" right after shopping somewhere new? That's AI at work. The system analyzes your typical spending habits, for example, where you shop and how much you spend, and flags anything out of the ordinary. Suppose someone suddenly tries to charge a big purchase in another country or buys gift cards in bulk with your card. In that case, the system can freeze the transaction or alert you instantly. These protections have gotten sharper over the years because AI learns from millions of real cases, constantly refining its sense of what's normal for each person. This vigilance means fewer headaches for you and less chance of dealing with fraud fallout.

To keep things balanced, it's smart to check how much of this personalization actually benefits you and where it might cross into feeling invasive. Most shopping sites let you manage your ad preferences or review the list of recommended products tied to your account. Take a moment to poke around the privacy or settings section on Amazon, Target, or any site you use regularly. You may be surprised at how granular these controls really are. Sometimes you can turn off certain types of tracking or clear your browsing history so old searches stop following you around. Understanding how AI shapes shopping isn't just about being a savvy consumer, it's about feeling more in control of what tech does behind the scenes. When you spot these patterns, it becomes easier to decide when to let AI lead the way and when to steer things back yourself.

---

***Try This: Tune Up Your Shopping Experience***

Open your favorite online shop or grocery app and look at the "Recommended for You" section. Do these picks match your real interests or feel off-base? Try changing your ad preferences (usually found under account settings or privacy options) and see if those changes stick the next time you log in. You might also check which ads show up after browsing for something unusual (like a gift for someone else) and note if suggestions shift accordingly.

---

## 2.6 SPOTTING AI—HOW TO TELL IF A TOOL OR SERVICE USES AI

Most of us use apps and devices every day without really thinking about what is going on behind the scenes. When a tool starts to feel like it understands you, such as a website suggesting articles you enjoy, that is usually AI at work. The first clue often shows up in small ways. Your phone's auto-correct might start using words you like, or your calendar may remind you about an event you barely remember adding. These moments are not accidents. They happen because AI is quietly learning from your habits and preferences.

Marketing is quick to use the word "smart" for many products, and while not every "smart" device runs on AI, it's a strong possibility. Look for words on packaging or ads like "learning algorithms," "personalized experiences," or "predictive" features. These aren't just buzzwords, they signal AI use. For example, "smart" photo albums sort by location or face, suggesting that AI is making choices on your behalf.

Automatic suggestions are another clear sign of AI at work. When your keyboard predicts the next word with surprising accuracy or your email app suggests how to finish a message, AI is quietly running in the background. Chatbots and voice assistants are even easier to spot. If a help window pops up with a friendly greeting or an assistant introduces itself—like "Ask Ava for support!"—you are almost certainly interacting with AI. These digital helpers reply instantly and stay consistent, unlike human agents who may vary in tone or timing.

Learning to spot genuine AI beneath marketing language is a useful skill. As artificial intelligence becomes part of everyday life, being able to recognize it keeps you informed and in control of how you use your technology. It is not about being skeptical, but about staying aware and empowered. When you understand what AI can do and how your data is used, you can decide which features are helpful and which ones you may want to adjust or turn off.

---

***Try This: Become an AI Detective***

Set a challenge for yourself: identify three apps or devices that improve or adapt as you use them. Note when and how they change. Did the feature exist before, or did it appear with more use? Check support or about pages for any reference to AI or machine learning. You'll likely discover many everyday tools quietly running on advanced tech.

---

# CHAPTER 3
# HOW AI "THINKS"
## STEP-BY-STEP LESSONS WITH VISUALS

### 3.1 HOW AI LEARNS—THE RECIPE ANALOGY FOR TRAINING DATA

Have you ever heard of someone making the mistake of using baking soda instead of baking powder? That classic baking blunder is actually a great way to understand how artificial intelligence "learns." Teaching an AI is like following a recipe in the kitchen. If you can picture yourself making a new dish, you're halfway to understanding AI's learning process.

Imagine you're about to bake cookies. The recipe is important, but the real difference comes from the ingredients—flour, sugar, eggs, and chocolate chips. In AI, these "ingredients" are the training data. Just as you select the best baking ingredients, providing AI with high-quality, varied data helps it perform well.

Now, think about what happens if your ingredients are stale or all the same, like using only salt. The cookies will taste terrible. Similarly, if AI is trained with biased, incomplete, or poor-quality data, the results turn out wrong. For example, suppose an AI is only shown pictures of golden retrievers. In that case, it might assume every dog is one, or fail to recognize other breeds entirely. This is why diverse data matters.

AI's learning process is much like following a recipe for the first time. You mix the ingredients, bake your first batch of cookies, and then taste them. If it is not quite right, you tweak the recipe.. Each batch is like another training cycle for AI. It takes an initial guess, tests it against reality, and adjusts based on feedback.

Feedback in baking comes from taste. For AI, feedback means comparing predictions with real answers. If it's right, great; if not, it adjusts its internal "recipe" and tries again. Picture baking several batches and noting that batch three was too flat, so you add more flour. AI does the same, running through thousands or millions of samples, refining itself with each try.

Improvements depend on honest feedback. If you taste cookies while congested or only ask one picky eater for comments, you learn little. For AI, if feedback lacks diversity, it won't actually improve or may even head in the wrong direction.

***Visual Flow: The Recipe Cycle***

Here's a simplified flow for both baking and AI learning:

**Ingredients (training data) → Recipe (instructions) → Baking (training) → Tasting (checking predictions) → Adjusting (learning from errors) → Re-baking (retraining with improvements)**

Each time through this cycle, both bakers and AI refine their outcomes. Burnt or bland cookies aren't failures—they're information for smarter tweaks next time. This loop continues until the results are good enough for real-world use.

Even with great ingredients and careful alterations, no batch is ever perfect every time. A cookie may spread too much or be crispier than usual. In AI, models sometimes stumble with tricky or new examples. That's why ongoing feedback is essential—just like taste-testing every batch makes your cookies better. Continuous feedback helps AI stay useful.

What makes AI effective isn't only smart programming. Its real strength comes from combining the correct data with constant cycles of practice, feedback, and refinement. When you hear that an AI is "learning," think of it like cooking—gathering ingredients, following a recipe, and adjusting the flavor as you go until the result is just right.

## 3.2 WHAT'S AN ALGORITHM?—SIMPLE STEPS BEHIND EVERY AI DECISION

Algorithms can sound intimidating, but honestly, you've probably followed dozens already today. Think of an algorithm as a set of instructions—plain and simple. It's like your morning ritual: wake up, turn off your alarm, brush your teeth, make coffee, check the news. You don't even have to think about it; you move from one step to the next. An algorithm is built on that same logic. It solves problems by guiding you through steps in a particular order. No need for fancy math or technical jargon—think of it as a reliable checklist for getting things done.

AI depends on algorithms to make choices. Picture being hungry and deciding to make a sandwich. You first check for bread. If it is available, you go on to the next step and add the filling. If it is not, you head out to buy more before continuing. That is an example of an "if-then" flow. Algorithms take large problems and break them into smaller steps, with each action depending on the result of the one before it. AI follows these logical flows all the time. Even sorting through your mailbox works the same way. If an envelope says "urgent," you open it immediately. If it looks like junk, you throw it away. If it is a bill, you place it in the pile for payment. The strength of algorithms lies in this predictability because they always follow clear steps rather than guessing.

AI algorithms do more than move through routine tasks. They make decisions that resemble quick judgment calls, though they rely on logic rather than instinct. The process is built on repeated "if then" steps that refine the outcome each time the instructions are carried out. Take an email spam filter as an example. The system examines each message for signals such as specific words, suspicious links, or patterns that frequently appear in unwanted mail. If enough warning signs are found, the email is placed in the spam folder. If not, it passes into the inbox. The filter is not guessing. It applies rules learned from analyzing countless real messages, which makes its choices consistent and dependable.

Think about movie recommendations next. You finish a romantic comedy on a streaming app, and suddenly, more rom-coms bubble up on your homepage. The app's algorithm isn't reading your mind—it's using your viewing history as input. It checks: if you liked "You've Got Mail," then suggest "Notting Hill." If you often stop watching thrillers after ten minutes, those kinds of movies start showing up less. The algorithm weighs what you watch, how long you stick with it, even when you pause or rewind certain scenes. Bit by bit, it builds a list of suggestions tailored to your tastes.

Visualizing algorithms can really help cement this idea. Let's picture making a sandwich:

**Start —Do I have bread?**

- **If Yes → Then Add contents → Eat sandwich.**
- **If No → Go to store → Buy bread → Then Add contents → Eat sandwich.**

Every arrow leads somewhere clear; every "if" has a "then." That's how algorithms keep things organized and predictable, which is why AI leans on them for all kinds of decisions.

What's powerful is that AI algorithms can handle way more complexity than our daily routines. Sorting digital photos? The algorithm might check for faces, locations, dates, and even lighting to group similar shots together or flag blurry ones for deletion. In business, AI algorithms might sort through sales numbers: if last month's revenue dropped below a set target, then alert the manager; if not, keep monitoring as usual.

The design of these algorithms is central to building trust and clarity. Because they follow clear steps rather than improvising, their behavior is consistent and easier to explain. This matters when you want to know why a specific email was filtered out or how a playlist was created for you. In many cases, AI relies on multiple layers of algorithms working together. One might scan subject lines in emails, another might evaluate the sender's reputation, and another might examine attachments. All of these processes combine like the gears of a clock to produce a smooth result.

Even more advanced systems stick to these core principles. For example, self-checkout machines in stores run through a checklist: scan item; if barcode matches database, list price; if weight doesn't match expected value for that item, flag for employee assistance. Each step branches into another action depending on the input—no guesswork involved.

What stands out is how these instructions shape everything from simple daily tasks to complex digital operations. Algorithms don't get distracted or forget steps. They don't skip brushing their teeth or miss making coffee unless something in their checklist says so. That reliability is what makes them vital to AI's role as your digital helper.

When you strip away all the high-tech language and look at the nuts and bolts, algorithms are just like any routine or habit—clear steps that turn "what should I do next?" into "here's what happens now." Whether sorting emails or picking movies, these instructions are at the heart of every smart decision AI makes.

## 3.3 NEURAL NETWORKS AS CITY TRAFFIC—A VISUAL WALKTHROUGH

Imagine a city map on a busy morning, filled with streets and intersections. Think of a neural network as a city for data instead of cars, where each neuron acts like an intersection guiding the "traffic" information throughout the system.

Picture a data point, such as a photo or text, as a car arriving at the city's edge, and the input layer, the first neighborhood. From there, the car travels through a network of streets and intersections known as hidden layers before reaching the final neighborhood, the output layer. Each neuron (intersection) in the hidden layers checks the data, makes a simple "turn left" or "right" type of decision, and passes its result to the next neuron. Each intersection only sees its local task, not the whole route.

As data moves through the intersections, the chosen routes come from what the network has learned so far. Some paths flow easily, others are slow due to weak or few connections. Early on, traffic is inefficient: data gets stuck or takes odd detours. With time and feedback, AI determines which intersections are most important, widening or shrinking "roads" between them. Each neuron adjusts how much it influences passing information. If an intersection (neuron) regularly leads to the wrong result, its influence is reduced for future traffic.

Hidden layers are like city districts, each specializing in specific tasks. One might focus on colors, another on shapes, another on textures—for image data. Data consistently flows through these districts, gathering clues at each stop. When data reaches the output layer, the network has combined those clues for its best prediction.

As the city begins to learn, imagine the first day of rush hour. Drivers choose random routes, creating confusion and heavy traffic. The network receives feedback showing that cars are not reaching their destinations efficiently. Using this information, it starts to adjust by suggesting faster routes and closing confusing roads to keep traffic moving more smoothly. With thousands or millions of training examples, data eventually finds the smoothest routes through the network.

Sometimes, unexpected "construction" or "accidents" (unusual data) crop up. Initially, too many cars may get routed through a single intersection until the network notices repeated problems and redistributes the flow. This adjustment process is continuous.

Imagine a diagram showing cars (data) entering from different city limits (the input layer), weaving through intersections (neurons), with some routes overcrowded (where mistakes happen) and others unused. At the end, cars exit into various neighborhoods (output classes). The city planner (training process) keeps changing which intersections matter most, continuously improving accuracy and efficiency with every trip.

This dynamic map enables neural networks to excel in tasks such as face recognition, language translation, or music recommendation. Every correct or incorrect outcome updates the city's layout, just as drivers learn from traffic jams. If an intersection appears unfairly selective, allowing only certain cars through, the AI adjusts to ensure information receives fair treatment and accurate decisions are made.

If you've ever wished for smarter traffic signals, you already grasp why neural networks need frequent updates and feedback. The more diverse and frequent the "traffic," the better the system learns to route information quickly and accurately.

## 3.4 SUPERVISED VS. UNSUPERVISED LEARNING—SORTING AND SOLVING PUZZLES

One way to explain how AI learns is to think about sorting laundry. Most of us have spent at least one Sunday afternoon pulling socks from a tangled mess. Now, picture two different ways to deal with that pile. In one case, someone has carefully labeled every sock: blue stripes, belongs to Jamie, or red polka dots, belongs to Alex. Matching them is a breeze. You look at the label and chuck it in the right drawer. That's supervised learning in a nutshell. The AI is handed labeled examples like photos of cats marked "cat," photos of dogs marked "dog." It learns by looking at these clear matches, figuring out what features (ears, snouts, fur patterns) go with each label. Over time, the AI gets really good at telling cats from dogs because it's been shown so many labeled images—just like you'd become a sock-sorting champion if every sock in your basket came with a sticky note.

But life isn't always that organized. Sometimes you dump all your clean socks in a heap with no labels, just colors and patterns staring back at you. No one's told you which pair goes together; you're left to figure it out based on what looks similar. Welcome to unsupervised learning. In this mode, AI doesn't get answers upfront. It simply analyzes raw data and groups similar items together. AI finds patterns and creates clusters, but it doesn't know for sure what those groups mean. It's like solving a puzzle with no picture on the box, just shapes and colors to guide you. In real life, this happens when AI looks at customer shopping habits without knowing who bought what. It simply finds groups—maybe "morning shoppers" versus "late-night snackers"—and helps businesses spot trends they never saw before.

The difference between these two learning styles is huge. Supervised learning is like having a teacher by your side. Every time the AI makes a mistake, the system says "nope" and helps adjust for next time. The feedback is immediate and clear. Over time, this cycle hones accuracy until the AI rarely misses a match.

Unsupervised learning doesn't have that luxury. No teacher steps in to say, "Nice job!" or "Try again." Instead, it relies on similarities (the way socks might share color or size) to form groups. There's no right or wrong answer—just clusters that may reveal hidden structure inside the mess. AI uses this technique to organize photos by face, even if it doesn't know the names attached to them. If your phone groups vacation photos by faces before you've tagged anyone, that's unsupervised learning quietly at work.

Both styles have strengths and quirks. Supervised learning excels when you have lots of clear answers. Unsupervised learning shines when you want to discover new trends or sort massive piles of data without much up-front knowledge.

***Quick Activity: Spot the Style***

Think about your favorite photo app or social media platform. When it suggests names for tagging, such as asking "Is this Sarah?", it is using supervised learning, which relies on labeled faces to make accurate suggestions. When the app creates albums of similar faces or organizes events without any input from you, it is applying unsupervised learning, grouping images based only on the patterns it detects. Take a moment to notice examples in your daily apps. Which ones seem to learn from clear answers, and which ones organize based on similarities? Once you start paying attention, you'll start seeing these two learning styles everywhere, and you'll know what to look for.

## 3.5 TESTING A FREE IMAGE RECOGNITION TOOL

There's nothing like rolling up your sleeves and seeing AI in action for yourself. Sometimes the fastest way to make sense of all this talk about data and patterns is to try out a real tool —no coding, no fancy equipment, just you, your web browser, and a couple of photos. If you've ever been curious about how computers can "see" and recognize what's in a picture, you're going to love this hands-on experiment. Grab your phone or jump onto your laptop, and open up Google's Teachable Machine (search for "Teachable Machine" and you'll find it). This website is a favorite for beginners because it skips the technical stuff and gets straight to the good part —playing around with AI that can look at images and try to guess what's in them.

Once you're on the page, choose the "Image Project" option. The site will prompt you to create a couple of categories. You might want to start simple: "Dog" and "Not Dog," or maybe "Coffee Mug" and "Water Bottle." If you have pets, snap a few photos with your phone or use some you already have. For each category, upload at least five or ten images. The more variety you include—different backgrounds, lighting, angles —the better your results. Be creative.

Now hit the "Train Model" button. This is where the tool starts to process the images you've uploaded, looking for similarities and differences between each group. It only takes a minute or two. Once it finishes, you'll see a preview window where you can test the model by uploading new images or using your webcam to show something live. Grab something unexpected—maybe a hat or a spoon—and hold it up to see what the AI thinks it is. Does it guess right? Does it get confused?

Pay close attention to how the AI responds when your image isn't exactly like the ones you trained it with. If you trained it on clear photos of your dog, but show it a blurry shot or introduce another animal, does it still guess "Dog," or does it get stumped? If you show it a picture of yourself holding a coffee mug, does it identify the mug—or does it guess something wild like "Not Dog"? This is where you start to see both the power and limits of AI tools.

You might notice that sometimes, the program makes hilarious mistakes. Maybe it calls your cat a coffee mug, or it's convinced your hand is actually a water bottle. Instead of getting frustrated, see these as learning moments. Every time the AI mislabels an image, ask yourself why that might be happening. Did your training photos all have similar backgrounds? Did they only show one angle? Was there enough variety in lighting and pose? Mistakes often come from too little data or from data that doesn't show enough range.

Sometimes, bias sneaks in without you realizing. If every "Dog" picture was taken outside, but all your "Not Dog" pictures were inside, the AI might start thinking that sunlight means "Dog." Or maybe there's an object that appears in every one of your "Not Dog" photos—a water bottle that shows up by accident every time—and suddenly the model associates that object with "Not Dog." This brings home just how easily AI can pick up on patterns we didn't mean to teach.

Now try uploading something that doesn't belong in either category like a plant or a book. Watch what the model does.

Most likely, it will still try to squeeze your photo into one group or the other, no matter how far off it is. Real-world AI works this way too: it doesn't know how to say, "I don't know," unless we specifically build in that option.

As you experiment, take a minute to jot down your observations. Which images did the AI nail? Which ones tripped it up? Did anything surprise you? You'll quickly see why building reliable AI takes lots of data and constant tweaking.

This little test packs in nearly every lesson about AI we've discussed so far: how important variety is in training data, how easily bias creeps in, and how feedback (even silly mistakes) helps us improve. It's also a reminder that while AI can do some pretty impressive things, it's not perfect—and sometimes its guesses are way off base. That's why human judgment still matters so much when we use these tools day-to-day.

## 3.6 FROM TRAINING TO INFERENCE—HOW AI GOES FROM LEARNING TO DOING

If you've ever played a sport, you know there's a big difference between practice and an actual game. Practice is where you get things wrong, try out new moves, listen to your coach, and repeat drills until you finally nail that technique. Game day, though, is where everything you've learned gets put to the test—there's no pausing to check the playbook, just reacting in real time. AI works pretty much the same way. During the "training" phase, an AI model gets exposed to all kinds of examples, making mistakes, getting corrected, and slowly getting better. It's repetitive, a bit messy, and involves lots of learning. You can picture it as endless scrimmage matches: the AI keeps adjusting after every move until it figures out which patterns lead to wins.

Once training wraps up, the AI switches into "inference" mode. This is like stepping onto the field for a real match. Now, instead of learning from feedback, the AI uses what it already knows to make decisions instantly—no extra practice reps, just quick responses. During inference, there's no coach whispering corrections in its ear. The AI sees new information—maybe a fresh photo or a sentence in another language—and makes its best call based on the patterns it practiced during training.

The real magic happens during inference. A translation app on your phone, already trained on millions of sentence pairs, can instantly turn a photo of a menu or a street sign into your language. It no longer needs to learn; it simply draws on what it already knows, recognizing patterns and delivering accurate translations in seconds. Behind the scenes, the app compares what you input to countless examples it has already processed, choosing the most likely meaning based on context. All the hard work happened during training, which is why the app can now respond so quickly and smoothly, almost as if it understands the language itself.

Still, every so often, you'll run into quirks. Occasionally, the app may convert a saying literally or misreads a blurry word on a sign. These errors remind us that even well-trained AI models have boundaries set by their original data and experiences. When something totally unexpected comes up, like a novel object in a photo or slang from a new region, the AI has to fall back on what it already knows.

Understanding how AI goes from endless practice to real-time action gives you more control when using smart tools in your own life. The leap from learning patterns behind closed doors to making split-second decisions out in the real world shapes everything from translations on your phone to identifying faces or sorting messages at work.

# MAKE A DIFFERENCE WITH YOUR REVIEW

## UNLOCK THE POWER OF GENEROSITY

*"The best way to find yourself is to lose yourself in the service of others."*

MAHATMA GANDHI

When you give without expecting anything back, something special happens. You feel better and maybe even inspire others along the way.

So, here's a quick question for you... would you help someone that you've never met?

That "someone" is a person who was just like you—curious, ready to learn, but not sure where to begin. They want to understand AI, but the world of algorithms and tools feels big and confusing.

Our mission at **Atwater Publishing** is simple: make artificial intelligence easy to understand and available to everyone. The only way we can do that is by reaching...well, everyone.

And this is where you come in.

Most people really do judge a book by its reviews. Your words can guide the next beginner, showing them that this book is worth their time.

Please help that future learner by leaving a review.

Your review:

- costs nothing
- takes less than a minute
- can make a real difference in someone's life

It's quick and simple: scan the QR code below and leave your review.

If you feel good about helping a stranger learn, then you're one of us. Welcome to the club.

Now, let's keep moving forward. The next lessons and hands-on activities are waiting for you, and they'll help you put AI into action faster and easier than you thought possible.

Thank you.

- **Atwater Publishing**

P.S. Here's something fun: when you share something useful with someone else, they see *you* as more valuable. So if you think this book could help a friend, send it their way.

# CHAPTER 4
# HANDS-ON AI
## PRACTICAL, NO-CODE EXPLORATION

### 4.1 TALKING TO CHATBOTS—CONVERSATIONAL AI IN ACTION

Ever wish someone could simply take care of the little things, like suggesting dinner ideas or reminding you of a birthday? That is precisely what chatbots are designed to do. Modern conversational AI feels friendlier and more natural compared to the older, frustrating customer service bots. You send a message to a chatbot as if you were texting a friend, and it responds within seconds, often with something useful or even a clever remark. Many people feel unsure at first, but after only a few minutes, it becomes clear that this is not science fiction. It is simply a tool that listens and replies, without requiring programming skills or technical knowledge.

Getting started takes very little effort. All you need is a web browser and a few minutes. With ChatGPT, visit OpenAI's website, create a free account, and you will see a chat box ready for your input. You can type something playful, such as "Tell me a joke," or something practical like "Help me make a shopping list." Press enter, and you will receive a response instantly. For Google Gemini, you may need to sign up for a waitlist, but once accepted, the process is just as simple. The Google AI site also provides a text box where you can type in your question or request. Both tools work in the same way: you write what is on your mind, and the AI responds.

Don't be shy—continue the conversation with follow-ups like, "What's a good dinner idea for tonight?" or "Explain how credit scores work." If an answer is unclear, type, "Can you make it simpler?" or, "Give me three quick tips." Chatbots remember the current conversation, making it easy to have an ongoing, contextual discussion. This makes them great for planning, learning something new, or just passing the time with fun trivia.

Still, chatbots aren't perfect. Although they can offer facts, jokes, and article summaries, sometimes answers are incorrect or a bit generic. Ask about very recent events—like this morning's news—and ChatGPT may give outdated info since its knowledge only goes up to a certain date. Sometimes bots miss the nuances of slang or humor and default to safe but bland replies. Specific or unusual questions, such as opinions on personal situations, often elicit generic, cautious responses. These flaws aren't dealbreakers. In fact, noticing both the strengths and the limits of chatbots can make using them a lot easier.

**Consider your needs:**

- **For creativity or nuanced text tasks:** ChatGPT is excellent.
- **For current events or web results:** Bing Chat is strong.
- **For account/order issues:** Customer service bots work best.

By experimenting with chatbots and testing their limits, you'll quickly learn their strengths, weaknesses, and how they can slot into your daily life.

***Interactive Exercise: Try Three Prompts***

Choose any chatbot (ChatGPT is beginner-friendly) and enter:

1. "Give me a five-day meal plan under $50"
2. "Suggest ways to relax after work"
3. "Teach me ten Spanish travel words"

Notice: does the bot handle your requests well? Does it use context or ask clarification questions? Note something that surprised you about its responses.

## 4.2 EXPLORING AI ART—GENERATING IMAGES WITHOUT CODING

The first time you open up an AI art generator, it feels almost like magic. You type a few words, hit a button, and in seconds, you get an image—something that's never existed before. No art school, no fancy software, not even a steady hand required. If you're curious but not sure where to start, you're in good company—plenty of us wonder if we're "creative" enough for these tools. The truth is, AI art doesn't care how much you've drawn before. All it needs is a prompt.

Pick a free online tool like Craiyon, DALL-E 2, or NightCafe. You'll see a simple search box, much like Google. To get rolling, think up a playful prompt. Try "a dog in a spacesuit," or get a little wild with "a futuristic cityscape at sunset." Enter your words and let the AI do its thing. Within half a minute, you'll usually see a grid of images—each a different spin on your idea. Sometimes they're spot-on, other times hilariously odd. If you want more structure, some tools ask you to pick an art style too: "cartoon," "oil painting," "watercolor." Just select what grabs your fancy.

The mechanics behind text-to-image generation are surprisingly approachable once you break them down. The AI reads your prompt by picking out key words and phrases—like "dog," "spacesuit," and "moon"—then rummages through its digital memory, built from millions of pictures and captions it has learned during training. It doesn't copy existing images. Instead, it mashes up visual elements, patterns, and textures to produce something new that fits your description. The process is a bit like a chef inventing a dish from whatever's in the fridge: sometimes the result is gourmet, sometimes it's more mystery casserole. That unpredictability is part of the charm. You never quite know if your "futuristic cityscape" will look like a gleaming metropolis or something out of a wild sci-fi dream.

One of the best parts about these generators is how tiny edits to your prompt can shift the results. Swap "realistic" for "cartoon" and suddenly your cat is starring in Saturday morning animation instead of posing for National Geographic. Even changing a single subject—"cat in a spacesuit"—generates entirely new artwork. It's fun to run the same prompt twice and compare what comes out; the images often shift just enough to keep things fresh.

Try experimenting with subjects you love or wish you could draw yourself. Maybe you want to see "a peaceful forest in autumn" or "an impressionist painting of pancakes." The only real limit is your imagination—and sometimes the AI's own quirks. Every tool has its own personality, built from its training data. Some are better at landscapes, others excel at quirky characters or vibrant colors. You might notice hands look weird or faces blur together—AI still has trouble with certain details.

Beyond the fun and experimentation, there's an ongoing debate about what makes AI art unique and where boundaries should be drawn. Unlike human artists who bring personal stories, lived experience, and intention to their work, AI acts as a mirror for whatever you ask—no feelings attached, just pattern matching at scale. This raises the question: Is AI art really "yours"? Some platforms allow you to download and use what you create however you wish; others may impose limits on commercial use or require credit to the platform or the developers behind the tool.

Ownership is a fuzzy territory with AI-generated images because, technically, no single person drew the lines or mixed the colors by hand. If you use an image for personal projects—a greeting card for Grandma or a background for your phone—you're likely fine. For selling prints or logos, though, check each platform's rules carefully. Some creators worry about originality: since the AI learns from millions of existing artworks and photos, can it accidentally copy someone else's style too closely? Most current systems blend features so thoroughly that exact duplicates are rare, but this is still a hot topic among artists and copyright lawyers.

Ethics also come into play when thinking about crediting sources and respecting creative labor. If an AI generator gives you an image that echoes a famous artist's style or borrows recognizable elements from real-world art, consider how you use and share it. Many people choose to add their own edits or combine several outputs to create something distinctly personal—a middle ground between pure machine-made art and human touch.

If you find yourself hooked by the surprise factor and creative freedom, keep pushing boundaries. Each click is another brushstroke in this new world of digital creativity—no coding, no pressure, just pure exploration and fun.

## 4.3 VOICE ASSISTANTS—CUSTOMIZING ALEXA, SIRI, AND GOOGLE ASSISTANT

Voice assistants like Alexa, Siri, and Google Assistant are everywhere—on your phone, your speakers, maybe even your TV or car. They're not just for asking trivia or setting timers, though. You can make them uniquely yours. Imagine waking up to your favorite playlist, hearing a weather update before you even open the curtains, or having your lights turn on with a single word. Setting up these routines is straightforward, and you don't need to know anything about coding. Open the app for your assistant—Alexa app for Echo devices, Google Home for Google Assistant, or your iPhone's Settings for Siri. Look for "Routines" or "Shortcuts." Start with something simple: a "Good Morning" routine. Choose a trigger phrase like "Good morning," then stack actions—have it turn on a lamp, read the news, and tell you your first appointment of the day. For reminders, say, "Remind me to take my medication at 8 PM," and it's set. If you want to personalize news and weather, select your favorite topics or local sources in settings; now you'll get headlines that actually interest you, not just random stories.

Automating other daily tasks can make life noticeably smoother. Try creating a shopping list by saying, "Hey Google, add eggs to my shopping list." The list syncs to your phone or smart display, so you always have it handy when you're at the store. You can also program smart lights (if you have compatible bulbs) to turn on when you get home or dim for movie night. In the Alexa app, tap "Devices," add your smart bulb, then set a routine: "When I say 'movie time,' dim lights to 30%." For busy mornings, program a voice command that checks your calendar and drive times for you. On Siri, set up a shortcut like "What's my day?" and it'll read out your schedule and reminders. Once you get the hang of the basics, try combining actions: have coffee brewed as the lights come on, or play relaxing music when it's time to wind down.

Privacy matters when using voice assistants—these tools listen for their wake word and sometimes store recordings. It's wise to review your privacy settings once in a while. In the app's privacy menu (or device settings), you can see what recordings have been saved. Delete anything you don't want stored with a tap. Most assistants let you set them to automatically erase recordings after a certain number of days. Adjust permissions for what personal info each assistant can access. For example, decide if Google Assistant can read your emails or calendar details, or if Alexa can access your contacts. Keeping tight control here means fewer surprises later and more peace of mind.

Sometimes, voice assistants don't get things right—misunderstandings happen often enough to be annoying. If your accent or phrasing isn't recognized, try re-training the device in the settings menu; most assistants have an option to "improve recognition" by learning how you speak. For example, if Alexa keeps struggling with specific names or words in your commands, add those as custom routines with alternative spellings or pronunciations (sometimes typing them in helps Alexa learn). If the device keeps picking up commands from TV shows or someone else in the house, move it farther from speakers or set up "voice profiles" so it knows who's talking.

When devices ignore requests or misinterpret what you say, patience helps. Repeat your command slowly and clearly; change phrasing if needed. If Siri won't recognize a family member's name, go into Contacts and use the "Add Phonetic Name" field. This little trick works wonders for hard-to-pronounce names. For recurring errors like smart lights not turning on, check that both your assistant and the device are updated and connected to the same Wi-Fi network.

**Here's a quick troubleshooting guide for those sticky moments:**

- Check Wi-Fi is strong and stable.
- Make sure all devices and apps are updated.
- Use clear, straightforward phrases ("Turn on kitchen lights" instead of "Could you please light up the kitchen?").
- Restart both the assistant and any connected devices if things go haywire.
- If all else fails, reset routines or re-link devices in the settings.

Voice assistants seem almost magical when they work right, but they're not mind readers—they rely on how we set them up and how we speak to them. Play around with routines and settings until things feel just right for you. Don't be afraid to test new ideas or ask your assistant for help troubleshooting —most can walk you through fixing common problems. With a bit of patience and customization, these AI-powered helpers really can take some of the stress out of your daily routine, letting you focus on what matters most to you.

## 4.4 SPOTTING DEEPFAKES—HANDS-ON WITH AI-GENERATED MEDIA

Deepfakes have become one of those buzzwords you hear everywhere, but the reality is even more wild than it sounds. Imagine watching a video of a famous politician saying something totally out of character, or hearing a celebrity's voice in an audio clip that just doesn't feel right. Deepfakes are AI-generated media—videos, images, or audio—that have been manipulated to swap faces, change voices, or even generate entirely new scenes. It's not just celebrities who are targets. Anyone with a social profile could, in theory, have their image or voice mimicked by these advanced tools. The process behind it isn't technical for the end user. With a few clicks, an app can paste someone's face onto another body or clone a voice reading words that person never actually spoke.

Maybe you've seen those funny videos where actors swap faces, and suddenly you're watching a comedy sketch with the wrong head on the right body. But there's a serious side too. Deepfakes can put words in someone's mouth, create fake news clips, or even trick people into thinking a loved one is asking for help. It's no wonder folks feel uneasy about what's real online anymore. The AI behind deepfakes uses neural networks—those same city-traffic models we talked about earlier—to map facial expressions frame-by-frame and blend them onto another person's face. The result can be eerily convincing, especially at first glance.

If you want to see how deepfakes work, try out a free detection tool like Microsoft Video Authenticator or Deepware

Scanner. You can upload a video or photo and let the app scan for signs of manipulation. Here's how it typically works:

1. Find a short sample video.
   - Many websites offer safe to use deepfake examples.
2. Save the video to your device.
3. Upload the video to the detector's website.
4. Wait a few seconds while the AI analyzes the video.
   - It looks for clues such as pixel inconsistencies or unusual blending around the edges of faces.
5. Review the results.
   - Most tools display a probability score (for example, "89% likely to be fake").
   - Suspicious areas are usually highlighted in red or yellow.

You don't always need fancy software to spot trouble. Some classic red flags give away an AI-altered clip. Let's break down the telltale visual and audio cues that can help you spot manipulation without any special tools.

**Deepfake Detection Checklist**

- Look for blinking patterns that don't match normal human behavior.
- Check for odd lighting, with parts of faces too bright or too dark.
- Listen for voices out-of-sync with mouth movement.
- Scan for fuzzy outlines around faces or hair that "melts" into backgrounds.

- Note accessories (hats, glasses) that pop in and out strangely.
- Watch jaw and cheek movement—does it look rubbery or mask-like?

Social and ethical issues swirl around deepfakes, making them more than just a technical curiosity. People worry about misinformation: doctored clips can damage reputations, influence elections, or spread rumors faster than ever before. There's also the risk of identity theft—scammers might use your face or voice in phishing schemes, tricking friends or coworkers into handing over private info or money. Because deepfakes can look so real, it's easy for false information to spread before anyone checks the facts.

The rule of thumb? Don't automatically trust what you see or hear online, especially if it seems shocking or out of character for the person involved. Before sharing anything that raises your eyebrows, pause and try to verify it. Tools like Google Images or TinEye use a reverse image search to see if a video appears elsewhere online with a different context. Ask yourself: Does this clip come from a reliable source? If something feels off, it probably is.

Learning to spot deepfakes is less about becoming an expert and more about building good habits. The more you practice noticing those little tells—odd blinks, awkward lighting—the better equipped you'll be to tell fact from fiction. And with AI evolving fast, staying cautious and curious might just be your best defense.

## 4.5 BUILDING A PERSONAL AI CHEATSHEET—YOUR QUICK REFERENCE TOOLKIT

Learning new tech often becomes much easier with the right cheat sheet and it can save time and frustration. AI is no different. With all the new terms, shortcuts, and real-life triggers, it's easy to get lost. Keeping a simple, personalized cheat sheet handy can provide confidence when encountering something unfamiliar or when a quick reminder is needed. Think of it as a private "AI decoder ring." It's not about memorizing everything; it's about having quick recall when it matters most..

Start by grabbing a blank page and giving it a title—"**My AI Cheatsheet.**" Leave some space in the margins for side notes or quick thoughts that pop up later.

Next, divide the page into clear sections:

- **Key AI Terms**
- **Visual Cues**
- **Everyday Triggers**
- **My Tools & Reminders**
- **Key Privacy Steps**

In the **Key AI Terms** section, jot down the words that seem to come up over and over again—like *algorithm, training data, inference,* and *prompt.* For each one, write a short, plain-language definition in your own words.

- Example: *Algorithm = step-by-step instructions for solving a problem.*

You could also add a small visual icon next to each term to help it stick:

- Gear for *algorithm* ⚙️
- Stack of books for *training data* 📚
- Lightbulb for *inference* 💡
- Speech bubble for *prompt* 💬

If you're more of a visual thinker, create your own symbols instead. The key is to make the page something your brain instantly connects with—your personal, easy-to-read "AI decoder ring."

For "**Visual Cues**," list the icons or labels you often see in apps or online. When you spot "Recommended for you" under a playlist or product, that's AI at work—write that down. Maybe add a shopping cart or magnifying glass symbol. If you get a fraud alert on your phone or see auto-correct fix your typo, mark those too. These little reminders help connect abstract AI concepts with concrete moments from your day.

"**Everyday Triggers**" is where you write down real-life situations that signal AI is behind the scenes. For instance, if your streaming app suggests a new show based on what you just finished watching, jot that down: "Netflix suggests shows = AI noticing my habits." Or when your phone's map app reroutes you and says "Faster route found," make a note—this is algorithmic traffic prediction doing its thing. If you use voice-to-text, write: "Phone transcribes my words = AI speech recognition." These triggers act as gentle nudges to notice how often AI quietly helps out.

You could also personalize the cheatsheet with your favorite tools and safeguards. Add a section titled "**My Favorite AI Tools**" and list the apps or features you actually use—maybe it's Spotify's playlists, Google Photos' automatic sorting, or Grammarly catching grammar slips in emails. You'll be surprised how fast this list grows as you notice more tech around you.

It's also wise to carve out space for privacy and ethics reminders. Under "**Key Privacy Steps,**" write down easy actions: "Review app permissions monthly," "Delete old voice recordings," or "Check privacy settings on new devices." You could even add a little lock icon or shield for visual emphasis. For ethical use, try reminders like: "Fact-check before sharing AI-generated content," or "Respect others' privacy (don't use face recognition apps on friends without asking)." These cues help you use AI thoughtfully and responsibly.

The best part? This cheatsheet is more than just a solo tool—it sparks conversations and group learning. Bring it along to a team meeting if your workplace is rolling out new tech tools; it'll help everyone get on the same page.

A cheatsheet adapts as you do. Update it whenever you discover a new trick or shortcut. If an app changes its appearance or adds new features, take a photo of your sheet and update the digital copy accordingly. Don't stress over making it pretty—the real value is in having something that makes sense to you.

Your personal AI cheatsheet is there to keep you confident and curious, not overwhelmed. It's proof that even with all the buzzwords and updates flying around, you don't have to remember everything—you just need the right prompts to jog your memory and help others along the way.

## 4.6 QUICK QUIZ—TEST YOUR AI AWARENESS WITH EVERYDAY SCENARIOS

Now that you have explored the practical side of AI, it is time to notice how often these invisible helpers show up in everyday life. Up next is an easy challenge to spot the ways artificial intelligence is already shaping the world around you. This is not about tricky questions or putting anyone on the spot. It is simply a way to build confidence, one real world example at a time.

**Q:** Your phone buzzes with a message from the bank warning about suspicious activity on your card. Is AI at play?
**A:** Yes — AI scans for spending patterns and triggers alerts when something looks off.

**Q:** You get a weather forecast for your exact street but not your friend's neighborhood. Did AI help?
**A:** Yes — machine learning crunches data from sensors and satellites to personalize predictions.

**Q:** You buy a coffee and the cashier gives you loyalty points. Is that AI?
**A:** No — that's automated but not true AI, just a basic rule-based system.

**Q:** You upload a photo and the app instantly tags friends' faces. Is that AI?
**A:** Yes — that's facial recognition, powered by AI models trained on countless images.

**Q:** You're typing an email and suggested words pop up as you write. Is this AI?
**A:** Yes — those smart suggestions come from language models that analyze how people write and predict what you'll say next.

**Q:** You're browsing a streaming app and it queues up a playlist "just for you." Is that AI?
**A:** Yes — AI reviews your listening history, finds patterns, and recommends music tailored to your tastes.

**Q:** Your fitness app suggests a new workout based on last week's activity. Is AI involved?
**A:** Yes — the app adapts using your data.

**Q:** You receive an automatic email when your bill is due. Is that AI?
**A:** No — it's simple automation, not learning or adapting.

**Q:** A grocery app recommends recipes using items already in your cart. Is AI involved?
**A:** Yes — this uses pattern recognition and data analysis.

For each question, let's break down why it matters.

1. Fraud alerts? Banks rely on machine learning to catch weird spending faster than humans could.

2. Weather predictions? AI sifts through endless streams of data in seconds.
3. Loyalty cards? That's more automation than intelligence.
4. Face tagging? Deep learning shines at matching unique features, even in group shots.

The more you practice spotting AI in action, the easier it gets to separate what's genuinely smart from what's simply automated. Over time, you'll find yourself noticing new examples everywhere—sometimes in places you least expect.

Remember: awareness is key to using AI wisely and responsibly. You're building not only knowledge but also sharp instincts for what technology can and can't do for you. Now, let's look at ways to bring these skills into the workplace and daily life so that AI becomes less of a mystery and more of an ally in whatever goals matter most to you.

# CHAPTER 5
# AI AT WORK
## UNLOCKING EVERYDAY PRODUCTIVITY

### 5.1 AUTOMATING REPETITIVE TASKS—AI TOOLS FOR BUSY PROFESSIONALS

If you've ever looked at a stack of paperwork or a long list of repetitive computer data and thought, "There's got to be a smarter way," you're not alone. Many people spend hours each week moving information, filling forms, or double-checking details that rarely change. It's tiring and makes the workday feel longer. AI-powered automation tackles these tedious chores so you can focus on higher-value work. The best part? No coding skills are needed.

A new wave of no-code AI tools makes automation accessible to everyone. Platforms like Zapier and IFTTT use easy drag-and-drop or recipe-style builders, helping you link your favorite apps, emails, spreadsheets, project boards without any programming. For instance, you can set up workflows like moving email attachments to a Google Drive folder or copying calendar events into a spreadsheet. You select triggers and actions, and the tool does the rest. Even if you're new to automation, these services walk you through each step clearly.

Say you spend time each day copying names and dates from an online form into a spreadsheet. With Zapier, you can create a "Zap" so every time a form is submitted, Zapier automatically transfers the data. No more copying and pasting or switching tabs. This saves minutes per task, which can add up to hours each week.

AI can also be very beneficial in document management. If your job involves handling invoices or receipts, then you know paperwork can pile up. Tools like Expensify use AI to scan and extract details from receipts. Just snap a photo and Expensify pulls out the merchant, amount, date, and organizes everything automatically. This reduces manual data entry and helps you catch errors before they become problems.

Reporting is another area where automation pays off. Weekly summaries and pulling together numbers can be a drag. Still, many automation tools now include AI-powered reporting that collects and summarizes data from different sources for you. Platforms like Google Looker Studio, Microsoft Power BI, and Tableau can automatically generate clear dashboards and summaries. Tools such as Zapier and HubSpot let you set triggers so reports appear when milestones are reached. At the same time, Notion AI and ClickUp can provide daily summaries of your key metrics on a set schedule.

Here's a practical scenario: Suppose you want to automate meeting notes from Zoom calls by saving recordings and transcripts directly into Google Docs. Start by linking Zoom and Google Drive in Zapier. Set the trigger (new Zoom recording) and the action (create and update a Google Doc with the meeting title and transcript). Zapier guides you through step by step, managing permissions and details. Once done, every Zoom call generates a Google Doc note automatically, saving you time and effort.

Automating routine digital chores isn't about replacing people; it's about reclaiming time and energy for meaningful work like brainstorming, connecting with clients, or just taking a well-earned break. These tools lighten your load so you can focus on what matters most.

---

***Interactive Element: Automation Reflection Exercise***

List three weekly tasks at work or school that drain your time—like sorting emails, updating spreadsheets, or logging expenses. For each, ask:

- Is it a clear, repeatable process?
- Is it predictable?
- Is it done often?

If so, these are great for automation.

Start small—try automating just one low-risk task with a tool like Zapier or IFTTT. Most offer free basic features. If it works, slowly expand to other areas. Not every task needs automation, but even small gains can add up.

---

## 5.2 AI FOR TEAMS—COLLABORATIVE TOOLS THAT MAKE MEETINGS SMARTER

Meetings can feel like a mixed bag. Sometimes they're energizing and productive, but other times, they drag on with tangents and missed details. If you've ever left a meeting unsure about next steps or realized later that you missed something important, you're in good company. This is where AI-powered meeting assistants and collaborative tools can genuinely change the game for teams of any size or background.

Picture this: You kick off a team call, and an AI assistant like Otter.ai quietly starts transcribing everything in real time. No frantic note-taking, no scrambling to remember who said what. Otter captures the entire conversation, labeling speakers and generating a searchable transcript. It even identifies key topics as you go along. The result feels almost magical—a complete record that you can review, search, and share with anyone who missed out. You can jump right to the moment someone assigned an action item or revisit where the group agreed on a deadline. These transcripts aren't just for record-keeping; they become useful documents, making it easier to double-check facts or clarify points if there's any confusion later.

### How to Use Otter.ai for Your Meetings

1. **Create Your Otter.ai Account**
   - Visit otter.ai on your browser or download the Otter app for iOS or Android.
   - Click **Sign Up** and choose a free or paid plan depending on your needs.
   - Complete the account setup with your name, email, and password (or sign in with Google/Apple).
2. **Connect Otter.ai to Your Meeting Platform**
   - From your Otter.ai dashboard, go to **Apps** or **Integrations**.
   - Link Otter.ai to your preferred platform (Zoom, Microsoft Teams, Google Meet).
   - Grant necessary permissions so Otter can join meetings as a participant or capture audio directly.
3. **Prepare Before the Meeting**
   - Ensure you have a stable internet connection.
   - Let all participants know Otter.ai will be recording/transcribing for transparency and privacy compliance.
   - If you're hosting, invite "Otter.ai" as a meeting participant or enable live transcription in your meeting tool.
4. **Start the Meeting and Enable Otter**
   - Join your meeting as usual.
   - Otter.ai will either:
     - Join automatically if you've scheduled it, or
     - Be started manually from the Otter app or browser.

   - Check that transcription has begun (you'll see live text scrolling in Otter).
5. **Follow Along in Real Time**
   - You can view the live transcription as the meeting happens.
   - Otter automatically labels speakers (if it recognizes voices) and highlights key terms.
6. **Review the Transcript After the Meeting**
   - Open your Otter.ai dashboard after the call.
   - Click on the meeting transcript to:
     - Search keywords (*e.g., "deadline," "budget"*).
     - Play back audio while reading the text.
     - Edit names, correct minor errors, or add context notes.
7. **Share and Collaborate**
   - Use the **Share** button to send the transcript link to teammates.
   - Export as text, PDF, or Word if needed for documentation.
   - Tag team members in comments to assign follow-ups directly in Otter.
8. **Use AI-Generated Highlights and Summaries** *(if available on your plan)*
   - View Otter's smart summary for decisions, action items, and deadlines.
   - Copy these summaries into your project management tools for quick task tracking.
9. **Store or Archive for Reference**
   - Keep transcripts in your Otter account for future reference.
   - Use folders in Otter.ai to organize by project, client, or team.

Now that you know the basics of using Otter.ai, here are some insider tips to help you work faster, capture more details, and get even more value out of every meeting.

### Pro Tips for Getting the Most Out of Otter.ai

**Name Your Meetings Clearly**
Give each meeting a descriptive title before or right after it starts so it's easy to find later.

**Train the Speaker Labels**
Correct speaker names in early transcripts—Otter will get more accurate over time.

**Highlight Key Moments in Real Time**
Click "Highlight" when important points come up so they're easy to revisit.

**Use Keywords for Faster Searches**
Tag transcripts with project names, deadlines, or keywords for instant retrieval.

**Integrate with Project Management Tools**
Copy action items into Trello, Asana, or Monday.com to keep tasks visible.

**Leverage the Mobile App**
Record quick, in-person conversations or brainstorming sessions—not just virtual calls.

**Archive Instead of Deleting**
Store older transcripts in labeled folders for future reference or audits.

AI meeting helpers go further by creating smart summaries that cut through the noise. Microsoft Teams, for instance, offers automatic recaps after a call ends. You don't just get a wall of text, you see highlighted decisions, clear action items, and deadlines pulled out from the discussion. These summaries help everyone stay on the same page, especially when conversations jump quickly between topics or when attendees join from different time zones. Nobody has to rewatch a whole meeting just to catch up because the most important parts are front and center. Teams can quickly assign tasks, follow up on loose ends, and avoid that awkward silence when someone asks, "Wait, who was supposed to handle this?"

Inclusivity gets a real boost from AI as well. Ever been in a meeting where you struggled with someone's accent or where technical terms flew over your head? Real-time transcription and translation in platforms like Zoom level the field for everyone. If someone joins from another country or prefers reading over listening, live captions make sure nothing gets lost. Some tools translate speech instantly into dozens of languages—so a team in Tokyo can work seamlessly with colleagues in Paris without missing a beat. For anyone who's hard of hearing or likes having written notes for reference, these features aren't just handy, they're game-changing.

There's something freeing about not having to scribble notes while trying to participate fully in the conversation. AI assistants allow you to focus on listening and contributing. Afterward, you can revisit the transcript for clarity, double-check what was agreed upon, and even search for keywords if you need specifics—like "budget," "timeline," or "next steps." This makes follow-ups smoother and saves everyone from the dreaded "what did we decide?" email chains.

AI isn't here to take over your meetings; it's here to make them more effective and inclusive. Whether you're a student working on a group project, a manager juggling remote teams, or someone who likes having clear records, these collaborative tools can lift some of the mental load so you can focus on what actually matters—solving problems together and moving projects forward.

---

***Try This: Team Evaluation Checklist***

After your meeting with an AI assistant, grab your team and run through these questions:

- Were all main points captured accurately?
- Did you notice any errors in speaker identification?
- Were action items clearly summarized?
- Did the transcript help anyone who missed part of the conversation?
- Was translation or captioning helpful for any attendee?
- Would you use this tool again? Why or why not?

Jot down each team member's experience and suggestions for improvement. You might discover that some people rely on transcripts to catch details they'd otherwise miss, while others like the instant summaries for quick follow-up. Sharing honest feedback helps you make smarter choices about which features to keep using and which ones need tweaking.

## 5.3 USING AI FOR SMARTER EMAIL AND CALENDAR MANAGEMENT

Email can feel overwhelming some days. You open your inbox and suddenly there are dozens—sometimes hundreds—of messages. Important notes from your boss, reminders for bills, newsletters you forgot you signed up for, event invites, and an occasional coupon for something you'll never buy. It can be overwhelming. But AI-powered email tools now give you a way to tame that chaos, sort what matters most, and cut down on the junk.

You might have noticed features like Gmail's Priority Inbox quietly working in the background. It's not just a fancy filter—it actually studies which emails you open, reply to, or ignore and learns what's important to you over time. Instead of dumping every message into a single pile, Priority Inbox splits your mail into sections: "Important and unread," "Starred," and "Everything else." That means you see the urgent stuff first and can ignore or delete the rest when you have time. If the system makes a mistake, it's easy to correct—just mark messages as important or not necessary, and the

AI learns from your feedback. It gets sharper the more you use it.

**Here's how to set up your Gmail inbox layout:**

1. Open Gmail
2. Click Settings
3. Under "inbox type," select:
    a. Default
    b. Important first
    c. Unread first
    d. Starred First
    e. Priority inbox
    f. Multiple inboxes

Another feature that's become a quiet lifesaver is Smart Reply. Sometimes you get an email that only needs a quick answer—"Thanks!" or "I'll get back to you soon." Instead of typing it out, Smart Reply suggests ready-to-send responses based on the message's tone and content. You still have control; simply use the suggestion as a starting point or personalize it before sending.

AI isn't just cleaning up email, though. Calendar management has gotten smarter, too. The days of endless back-and-forth messages ("Are you free Tuesday at 2?" "No, what about Wednesday?") are fading out. Now, tools like Calendly let you share your availability in a simple link. Colleagues or clients pick a time that works for them, and the app automatically blocks that slot in your calendar. No more double-booking or frantic last-minute changes. Outlook, on the other hand, has started suggesting meeting times as soon as you add invitees. So, even if you're scheduling with people in different time zones, it instantly finds overlaps.

You don't have to stop there. Filters and smart labels can take your email management even further. Start by creating custom rules. Most email platforms make this simple: select a message, choose "Create filter," and set conditions like sender, subject line, or keywords. Decide if you want those emails marked as important, starred, labeled, or moved straight out of your inbox. It's fast and flexible.

Take a few minutes to dig into your settings. If using Gmail, click the gear icon and head to "See all settings," then find "Notifications." You can choose to only get alerts for important mail or mute everything except calendar reminders. Outlook and other apps offer similar controls. If constant notifications pull your attention away, switch your phone or computer to Do Not Disturb during focused work sessions, allowing only essential alerts to come through.

Building an AI-powered workflow for yourself isn't about using every feature at once; it's about picking what makes your day smoother. Here's a Mini-challange:

- **Monday:** Turn on **Priority Inbox** or set up one email filter.
- **Tuesday:** Enable **Smart Reply** or try scheduling a meeting with **Calendly**.
- **Wednesday:** Adjust your **notification settings**.
- **Thursday & Friday:**
  - Check how easily you can find important emails.
  - See if meetings are easier to schedule.

Everyone has their own style when it comes to communication and organization, so don't be afraid to experiment until things feel right for you. The real magic is that these AI-powered features don't require big tech skills—they just need curiosity and a few minutes of setup time. Over time, what once felt like chaos starts to look more like order, giving you back hours each week for projects that matter.

---

***Checklist: One-Week Workflow Tune-Up***

- Did your inbox feel less stressful today than last week?
- Did you spend less time answering routine emails?
- Were meeting invites easier to handle?
- Did any urgent messages slip through the cracks?
- Did you have fewer interruptions from notifications?
- Were there any features that surprised you—in a good way?

If even one answer is yes, that's progress worth celebrating.

---

## 5.4 AI IN CUSTOMER SERVICE—CHATBOTS AND BEYOND

Picture yourself needing help with a lost bank card late at night or wanting to change a flight after hours with no agent in sight, phones on hold, and frustration building. Now, imagine landing on a website and a little chat window pops up: "How can I help you today?" You type your question, and within seconds, you get an answer. That's the power of AI chatbots working in real time. These bots don't sleep or take vacations. They handle thousands of customer questions at once. You can spot them everywhere—banking sites walk you through account issues, airlines help you change seats, and retailers track orders or process returns, all with an AI "helper" right there on the page.

What's wild is how these bots have gotten so much sharper. Early chatbots felt like talking to a wall—they'd spit out generic replies or get stumped by anything beyond a yes/no question. Modern versions utilize natural language processing, which enables them to pick up on context, slang, and even some spelling errors. Still, they have their limits. They're fantastic at answering FAQs, checking balances, processing simple requests, or resetting passwords. But if your problem is complex—like resolving a weird billing error—they often know when to pass you along to a real person.

Behind the scenes, AI doesn't just help customers directly; it also acts as a sidekick for human support agents. In busy help centers, tools like Zendesk's AI-powered ticket triage sort incoming messages by urgency, topic, and even mood—flagging angry or urgent cases for faster attention. AI scans each inquiry and suggests replies based on similar past tickets or company guidelines. It takes some of the mental load off the live agent and speeds up response times for everyone.

While bots handle routine questions, humans step in when things get tricky. If the chatbot can't solve your issue after a few tries, it doesn't just leave you hanging. Most systems have built-in escalation pathways, instantly looping in a real agent with all the chat history attached, so you don't need to repeat yourself. This tag-team approach means customers receive help faster, and staff can focus on problems that require genuine empathy or creative problem-solving. You get the best of both worlds: instant service for simple needs and expert attention for anything that requires a human touch.

---

***Try This Chatbot Experiment:***

Open any major retailer or airline website and look for the chat option. Some sites display an icon in the bottom corner. Click it and type a question like "Where's my order?" or "How do I reset my password?" Notice how quickly the bot responds. Test its range—ask about store hours, returns, or loyalty points. If you stray off script or get more specific ("My item arrived damaged and I want a replacement"), watch how the bot either offers more detailed steps or asks if you want to chat with a live agent.

---

Compare this to old-school customer service—long wait times, repeating your story on every transfer, or agents needing to dig for your info while you're on hold listening to elevator music. With AI in the mix, support feels more personal and less like an obstacle course.

Bots aren't here to steal jobs—they're here to make work less repetitive and offer more innovative experiences for everyone. If you've ever left an online chat thinking "Wow, that was easy," you've already seen this shift in action. Next time you reach out for help online, pay attention not just to what gets answered but how smoothly the digital and human support teams work together behind the scenes.

## 5.5 AI IN HIRING—RESUME SCREENING AND BIAS EXPLAINED

Artificial intelligence now plays a significant role in how companies hire. If you've applied online, chances are your resume was read by an algorithm—Applicant Tracking Systems (ATS) like Greenhouse or Lever—before a human saw it. These digital gatekeepers sift through resumes, quickly sorting and ranking applicants by matching them to the job description with keywords and phrases. This saves hiring managers time by surfacing a shortlist of candidates. But as efficient as this sounds, there's complexity underneath.

When you submit your application, an ATS scans your resume for keywords that align with the job ad (like "project management," "customer service," or "Microsoft Excel"). The system notes which words appear and how often. If your resume mirrors the language in the posting, you're much more likely to move ahead. Importantly, formatting impacts how well the ATS reads your information. A clean, simple layout using standard headings and bullet points helps the AI accurately analyze your resume. Graphics, fancy fonts, images, or unusual layouts can confuse the system, so stick to straightforward text.

However, automated screening can repeat hidden biases if left unchecked. If a company's prior hiring data favored certain genders or backgrounds, the AI may learn and perpetuate those preferences. Cases exist where gendered language or gaps in employment lead AI to overlook otherwise qualified applicants. For example, suppose most historic resumes show no career breaks. In that case, the system may filter out parents returning to work or people changing careers, even if they're strong candidates.

To address these issues, companies are starting to audit their algorithms for fairness, adjusting training data, and adding safeguards so non-traditional applicants aren't unfairly excluded. Some remove identifying information like names or addresses to reduce unconscious bias and focus more on a candidate's skills.

To help your application stand out for both humans and AI, use keywords from the job description in your resume, woven naturally into your experience and skills sections. Don't simply copy-paste, try to use the company's exact wording when relevant (e.g., if the posting says "team leadership," use that phrase). Stick to simple formatting and do not include tables, columns, images, or graphics. Use bulleted lists and clear section headings like "Experience," "Education," "Skills". Save your resume as a text-based .docx or PDF to make sure the file is readable.

Adding logos, graphics, or headshots might make your resume visually appealing, but these often confuse the algorithms so it is best to avoid them. Standard fonts and straightforward layouts help your resume get read correctly by both ATS and human reviewers.

If you're curious about a company's hiring tools, don't hesitate to ask during an interview or reach out to HR. A question like, "Does your hiring process use any automated screening tools or AI-driven assessments?" showcases your tech awareness and helps you understand how your application will be processed. Some systems even allow you to track your status or request feedback.

Doing some research in advance is also helpful. Many employers list their ATS on their careers page or in FAQs. If you know which system they use, you can look up resume optimization tips specific to that tool. Online tools can also preview how your resume might perform in an ATS, highlighting areas to fix.

Reflect on your own work history and potential biases. If you have gaps or role changes, frame those experiences positively and focus on the skills you gained. The goal is to show your strengths and to prevent algorithms from interpreting your background as a red flag.

Remember, while AI influences the sorting of resumes, actual people still make the final decisions. The objective is to clear the ATS filter so you can present your story and qualifications in person. Staying informed about AI's role in hiring lets you adapt your approach while keeping your individuality and honesty. As algorithms become more common in the workforce, learning to communicate with both machines and humans will remain an increasingly valuable skill.

## 5.6 YOUR AI CAREER ROADMAP—ENTRY PATHS FOR NON-TECHIES

Working "in AI" isn't just for software engineers or data scientists. There's a vast need for people who understand the basics of AI and can link those skills to roles beyond programming. Companies want team members who can bridge technology and real-world needs. They are looking for people who know enough to ask good questions, spot opportunities, and help their teams adapt. AI now plays a role in many kinds of work. Project managers use it to plan and track progress. Marketers turn to AI tools to spot trends and measure campaign success. Sales teams rely on AI insights to understand customers.

Whether you work in an office, school, retail, or healthcare, you're likely already using or will soon use AI-powered software. The key isn't learning to code, but developing "AI literacy" to understand what AI can and can't do, how to talk with tech teams, and how to use AI tools to make work smoother. For instance, marketers might use AI to target audiences or automate posts, while project managers can track project risks using intelligent dashboards.

You can start building your AI literacy now. Many free or affordable resources exist. The Elements of AI course, for example, is beginner-friendly and explains concepts in simple terms with hands-on exercises. LinkedIn Learning offers classes like "AI for Project Managers" or "AI in Marketing." Podcasts such as "AI in Business" or "Practical AI" cover trends in an easy-to-digest format—great for listening during commutes or walks. If you enjoy learning alongside others, consider joining online groups in your field that focus on AI—these often feature Q&A sessions and real-world case studies.

Employers seek people who can explain AI, recognize potential risks, and turn customer feedback into useful improvements. Backgrounds in teaching, sales, admin, or social work now lead to jobs as AI trainers, implementation specialists, or community managers.

Building an AI-focused career isn't about instant programming skills. It's about being open to new tools, connecting people with technology, and helping your team adapt. As you become more confident, new opportunities will appear and often in unexpected places.

Ultimately, the most valuable skill is understanding how AI fits into daily tasks, not just technical know-how. Whether it's making meetings smarter or guiding your team toward the best tool, each step increases your value.

---

***Checklist: Build Your Personalized Plan***

- Choose one AI tool to explore.
- Join an AI community group (online or in-person).
- Set and pursue a 90-day goal: complete a course or apply an AI feature at work.

Check in weekly to track progress, see what's working, where you're stuck, and adjust as needed.

---

# CHAPTER 6
# ETHICS, BIAS, AND PRIVACY
AI FOR RESPONSIBLE BEGINNERS

## 6.1 UNDERSTANDING AI BIAS—WHY IT HAPPENS AND HOW TO SPOT IT

AI bias is when an artificial intelligence system produces results that are systematically unfair, inaccurate, or unbalanced toward certain groups of people, ideas, or outcomes. This usually happens because the AI is trained on data that already contains human biases, or because of the way the system is designed and used.

**How AI Bias Shows Up**

- **Training data bias** – If the data used to train an AI is incomplete or unrepresentative, the system may favor some groups while overlooking others.
- **Historical bias** – If past decisions were unfair (for example, in hiring or lending), those patterns can carry over into AI models.

- **Cultural or language bias** – AI may perform better in certain languages or cultural contexts because it has seen more data from those areas.
- **Confirmation bias in design** – If the creators of an AI system make assumptions that favor one outcome, the system may reflect those choices.

### Why It Matters

AI is being utilized in critical areas such as healthcare, hiring, finance, policing, and education. If bias is not recognized and addressed, these systems can unintentionally reinforce discrimination or make unfair decisions at scale.

These aren't just technical glitches—they affect daily life. You might find an online form that won't accept your name due to an accent or a hyphen, or notice that a video call background filter works well for one person but not for you. These are subtle signs of AI bias and cues that the system isn't treating everyone equally.

### Spotting AI Bias—A Quick Checklist

- Do recommendations frequently favor one group or user type?
- Are results inaccurate or strange for people from different backgrounds?
- Is there a pattern of certain users being left out—missing suggestions or features?
- Does the system struggle with diverse names, accents, languages, or cultural references?

If you are noticing these trends, then you are likely seeing signs of AI bias. Knowing what to look for helps you respond. Does the tool work for everyone? Who tested it? What data was used for training? You don't need to be a specialist to ask these questions.

If something feels unfair, record the incident and take screenshots. Note who was affected and describe what happened. Reach out to customer support or IT with specifics. For example, "The app didn't recognize my name," or "This filter never works for me." Many platforms now provide easy ways to report such issues. If your workplace or school uses new AI tools, voice your concerns during roll-outs or email IT with your observations.

Small steps count. Asking whether fairness checks were done sends a message that equity is valued. Encourage the use of tools that share their bias-reduction steps or results from fairness audits.

Bias in AI often hides in invisible habits and built-in assumptions. The more you watch for it, the sooner you'll sense when something feels off. Think of bias like a funhouse mirror—distorting reality until someone points out the reflection doesn't look right and calls for change.

Fair technology must work for everyone—not just for those who fit into a particular pattern.

## 6.2 PROTECTING YOUR PRIVACY—SAFE AI USE AT HOME AND WORK

If you're like most people, you've probably had a moment where your device seemed to know you a little too well. Have you ever asked your smart speaker for a weather update, and the next day, it reminds you to bring an umbrella before you even leave the house? Or maybe you've noticed your health app nudging you to stand up after hours at your desk, tracking your steps, heart rate, and sleep patterns with uncanny precision. All of this is made possible by AI quietly collecting, storing, and sometimes sharing details about your routines, preferences, and habits. What feels convenient can also be a little unsettling when you pause and realize just how much is being recorded.

Voice assistants like Alexa, Siri, and Google Assistant are always "listening" for their wake word but often record snippets of conversation to improve accuracy or provide faster responses. These recordings are sometimes stored on company servers, not just on your device. This means someone might review clips to help the AI learn, or in rare cases, clips could be shared with third-party partners for technical improvements. Health trackers like your smart watch or fitness band, log sensitive data about your sleep, exercise, and even how stressed you feel. Many apps sync this data to the cloud, where it's analyzed by AI to give you personalized insights. But once information leaves your device, it's harder to control who can access it or how it might be used in the future.

The risks with AI-driven devices go beyond the obvious. Data isn't just collected, it can be combined and analyzed to infer things you haven't shared directly. For example, if your search history includes lots of late-night symptom lookups, then AI might guess you're dealing with insomnia or anxiety, even if you never told anyone. This type of digital eavesdropping isn't always sinister. Still, it does mean companies can piece together a profile that feels uncomfortably personal. Sometimes, AI-powered apps can even predict things like pregnancy or medical conditions based on seemingly innocent data points—like shopping habits or fitness levels. These inferences aren't always accurate, but can end up in marketing databases or be sold to advertisers who target you with specific ads.

You have more power than you think to protect your privacy and limit what AI systems know about you. The first step is continually reviewing the permissions on your devices. For smart speakers, open the app that manages your assistant (like Alexa or Google Home) and look for privacy settings. You'll usually find options to listen to, delete, or prevent the storage of voice recordings. Some apps allow you to set how long data is kept before it's erased automatically. On phones and tablets, check the permissions granted to each app. Many of them collect location information, microphone access, or contacts without an apparent reason. If an app doesn't need access to something, turn it off. Health and fitness apps often let you download or delete stored data through the settings menu. Don't hesitate to clear out information that feels too personal.

Managing what stays private is an ongoing habit. Make it part of your routine to check permissions every few months. Set a calendar reminder if that helps. Look for new settings after app updates since companies sometimes change default behaviors or add new data features without making them obvious. Use strong, unique passwords for every AI-enabled tool or service you use, not just the ones that seem most important. If your device supports two-factor authentication (like a text code or an authentication app), turn it on to add a vital extra layer of security.

---

***Privacy Checklist: Home and Work***

- Review device and app permissions at least quarterly; remove access for anything you don't recognize or no longer use.
- Regularly delete voice recordings and activity logs from smart speakers and search assistants.
- Download copies of your health or fitness data before deleting from apps if you want a personal record.
- Use unique passwords for every AI tool; don't recycle passwords across work and home accounts.
- Enable two-factor authentication wherever possible.
- Turn off location tracking for apps that don't need it.
- Watch for new settings after software updates—revisit privacy options when prompted.
- At work, ask IT how employee data is handled in new AI-powered tools; request documentation if privacy practices aren't clear.
- Never share sensitive work documents with AI chatbots unless your company has approved them.
- Talk with family members about privacy features on

shared devices, especially if kids or seniors use smart tech at home.

---

AI brings numerous benefits, but maintaining control is up to you. Getting comfortable with privacy settings and staying alert to changes helps ensure that your smart tools work for you—not the other way around.

## 6.3 BLACK BOX AI—WHY SOME DECISIONS ARE HARD TO EXPLAIN

Using AI often feels like dealing with a locked safe: you put in information and get a result, but the process in between remains hidden. This is what people refer to when they call some AI models "black boxes." Even creators of these systems frequently can't explain precisely how a specific decision was made. The issue isn't secrecy; it's that the logic inside complex algorithms, with millions of connections and layers, is deeply tangled and opaque. While you might expect engineers to point out the exact moment the AI made a choice, all they can often see is a dense web of mathematical patterns. Some answers are lost simply because the system's inner workings are too complex to map cleanly.

The black box problem isn't just technical—it can have real effects on daily life. For example, applying for a loan and being unexpectedly denied, with only a vague explanation like "the computer says no," is a frustrating outcome. You may do everything right, but still receive only generic feedback. Or, you notice your social media feed seems to predict your mood or interests, but can't tell why it shows certain posts and hides others. These systems rarely explain their logic; they just give you results shaped by hidden rules.

The stakes are even higher when black box AI influences major decisions, such as healthcare approvals, job screenings, or criminal justice recommendations. In these situations, trust is critical. Suppose you lose a job interview or medical test results because of an algorithm's decision. In that case, you naturally want to know what factors led to that outcome. Yet with modern AI, all anyone may see is a jumble of probabilities and pattern-matching, making transparency and accountability very difficult. Challenging or even understanding such decisions becomes almost impossible, leaving people with more questions than answers, which often feels unfair.

For organizations using these tools, opacity can erode trust. If they can't explain why you were denied a loan or why your resume was filtered out, customers and employees may feel alienated. Fairness isn't just about correct decisions—it's also about giving people understandable reasons for those decisions. In critical fields such as medicine or finance, being able to clearly explain outcomes is essential for true accountability.

So what should you do when an app, device, or service acts as a black box? The Answer: start by expecting explanations. If AI impacts essential parts of your life—finances, health, employment—ask vendors for plain-language summaries about how their systems work. For example, you can ask what data the AI uses or how it ranks candidates. Companies should be able to list key factors influencing outcomes, how data is weighed, and describe options for appeals.

When considering a new AI-powered tool, look for transparency. Do companies publish information about their algorithms? Is there a FAQ section that describes how your information is processed? You should know what happens with your data, whether a human reviews decisions, and how mistakes or appeals are handled. Vague or missing answers are a red flag.

If you get an unexplained outcome—like a mysterious bank charge detected by an AI fraud tool, or an unexpected social media block—reach out to support and request details. Ask, "Can you walk me through why this decision was made?" or "Can I appeal this result?" Many companies now have teams to address these questions. The more people demand clarity, the more companies are pressured to make their systems understandable.

If you're helping decide whether to use new AI tools at work, insist on testing and require documentation on how decisions are made. Look for features that let users review logs of AI actions. When possible, choose products that offer some "explainability"—such as visualizations or plain-English summaries, rather than just mysterious scores.

Living with black box AI doesn't mean surrendering control; it means staying curious and vocal about how technologies shape your experiences. Asking questions and providing feedback helps push companies toward AI systems that are not just intelligent but also understandable and fair for everyone.

## 6.4 AI AND FAIRNESS—TACKLING REAL-WORLD ETHICAL DILEMMAS

AI's reach stretches far outside the tech world—right into public spaces, our communities, and the workplace. Take facial recognition in city centers, for example. The technology promises security and convenience, such as catching suspects or locating lost people, but it also raises challenging questions. Who gets scanned? Is everyone treated equally, or do some groups get flagged more often? Imagine walking through a park and knowing a camera might be trying to match your face to a database, even if you're just out for a casual walk. Not everyone feels safe with this level of surveillance, and history has shown that these systems sometimes misidentify people. There is a risk of innocent people being wrongly accused, or simply feeling like they're always being watched. That's a heavy social cost.

Predictive policing uses algorithms to forecast where crimes might occur or who might reoffend, sometimes influencing decisions about bail or sentencing. It sounds efficient, but what if these predictions are based on flawed data—historical crime records that reflect social inequalities? Suddenly, AI isn't just making suggestions; it's shaping real lives and futures. These decisions can follow someone for years, determining whether they get a second chance or feel trapped by a system that never really saw them as individuals.

Ethical dilemmas like these seem overwhelming, but you can break them down with a simple framework. Ask yourself: Who benefits from this AI decision? Sometimes it's obvious —maybe a company saves money with automation—but who might be left out or even hurt? Are certain neighborhoods policed more heavily because an algorithm says so? Is every voice represented in the data and design process? The next step is to look for blind spots. If an AI tool claims to be "fair," dig into what that really means—fair for whom? An app that only works well for people with certain accents or backgrounds isn't fair in practice, no matter what the marketing says. You can also consider how feedback is collected and acted on; is there an easy way for people to raise concerns if something feels unjust?

It's essential to involve many voices in building and using AI, not just engineers or executives. For instance, translation apps have famously struggled with non-binary pronouns or languages outside the mainstream. When only a narrow group develops these systems, entire communities get overlooked. Developers didn't mean harm; they just didn't think about users outside their usual circles. The same thing happens with recruiting software that favors graduates from specific schools because the training data mainly contains resumes from those institutions. The result? Candidates from community colleges or international backgrounds get fewer chances—not because of their abilities, but because the system wasn't designed to see them.

If you spot these patterns at work or in your community, don't stay silent. Raising ethical questions doesn't make you difficult, it makes you responsible. You don't need to have all the answers; just starting the conversation can make a big difference.

Try using direct but open language when voicing concerns. Prompts to consider:

- "I've noticed that our new scheduling tool seems to overlook part-time staff when assigning shifts. Has anyone checked if it works equally well for everyone?"
- "I read that some facial recognition tools don't perform as accurately for all skin tones—do we know if ours was tested broadly before rollout?"

These questions aren't accusations; they're invitations to dig deeper together. Sometimes, sending an email feels safer than speaking up in a meeting. Here's a sample you could adapt:

> "**Hi** [ Name],
> **I've been learning about how some AI tools can unintentionally favor certain groups or leave out others. I'm curious about how we're making sure our new [tool or app name] is fair for everyone who'll use it—especially folks from different backgrounds. Could you share what steps have been taken to test for fairness or gather feedback from a wide range of users? Is there a process for people to report issues if they notice something off? Thanks for helping keep our tech inclusive.**"

Reaching out with a note like this gets the ball rolling without putting anyone on the spot or sounding confrontational.

Communities thrive when everyone feels seen and heard—not just the majority. By asking who stands to gain or lose from an AI decision, you help keep fairness at the center of the conversation. Whether it's challenging how policing tools are used in your neighborhood or questioning why a company's chatbot keeps stumbling over nontraditional names, your perspective matters. The most ethical solutions emerge from collective effort by listening to those most affected and ensuring their stories shape the technology we all share.

## 6.5 EVALUATING AI NEWS—SEPARATING HYPE FROM REALITY

Scrolling through your feed, you've likely seen AI headlines that sound straight out of science fiction—claims like "AI will steal your job by next year!" or "This new AI can think like a human!" It's easy to get pulled in by buzzy headlines or, just as easily, misled by hype, fear, or misinformation. If you've ever wondered whether a viral AI story is worth believing, or just more clickbait, you're not alone. The truth is, separating AI fact from fiction requires a bit of critical thinking, skepticism, and some practical habits.

When reading about AI, use a simple checklist:

- Does the story give concrete examples of what the technology can do?
- Are there real, named sources—such as researchers, universities, or companies—explaining the technology?

- Is evidence provided, such as peer-reviewed studies or real-life demonstrations?

Trustworthy stories point to specific projects, published results, or at least interviews with people directly involved. Watch out for vague statements like "experts say" without names or credentials; they often mean you should investigate further. Journalists can get swept up in excitement and skip details, but those details actually matter.

Some clues can tip you off when something sounds more like hype than fact. Big words like *miracle, doom, revolutionize,* or *destroy* are usually there to grab attention, not to share solid information. Watch out for headlines that promise instant results like "AI will cure cancer this year!" or stories shouting about a "breakthrough" with no real research to back it up. True discoveries usually bring cautious excitement from scientists, not overblown claims from marketing teams.

A classic sign of misinformation is when stories don't reflect real-world context. You might read "Self-driving cars are here!" but most cars you see on the street still have drivers. Even in places where self-driving cars are being tested, human safety drivers are common, and full deployment remains rare. Demos might look impressive, but they often skip limitations like restricted locations, weather, or special roads. If it sounds too good (or too scary) to be true, it's likely at least partially exaggerated.

Fact-checking is easier than you might think. If something doesn't sound right, search for the claim on reputable sites like MIT Technology Review, AI Now Institute, or The Gradient. These sources explain both what AI can do and what it can't, usually backed up by technical details. Fact-checking sites like Snopes or Media Bias/Fact Check can also quickly reveal if a story's been debunked or misrepresented. You don't need to be an expert. Often, just seeing what reliable sources say, is enough to avoid falling for hype.

Staying grounded doesn't mean ignoring real change. AI is reshaping industries but focusing on evidence over excitement helps you avoid panic and false hope. By looking for credible sources and details, you'll spot what's real, what's possible, and what's just hype designed for clicks.

---

***Try This: To get Savvier with AI News***

Next time you spot an eye-popping AI headline, pause before reacting. See if the article mentions specific people, credible organizations, or real data. Does it link to studies or offer a balanced perspective? Often, a quick scan for these markers can reveal exaggeration right away. If you're still unsure, look for respected science outlets and compare their coverage.

---

## 6.6 INSTANT ACTION—SIMPLE STEPS TO BE AN ETHICAL AI USER

Remember, being a thoughtful AI user isn't about knowing all the technical details—it's about the little things you do every day. Sometimes, it's as simple as pausing before you share something online. If an image or a story is created by AI, ask yourself, "Is this accurate?" or "Could this mislead someone?" A quick fact-check or reverse image search can stop the spread of misinformation before it starts. When you pass along AI-generated content, mention its source. That tiny habit gives others a heads-up and helps slow down confusion.

Look for tools that take the mystery out of decision-making. When an app explains why it suggests a product or how it sorts your photos, that's a good sign. Companies that value transparency usually care more about fairness and your privacy. You might see a settings menu labeled "Why did I get this result?" or a little info icon you can tap for details. If you don't see clear explanations, consider whether you want to keep using that service or if there's an alternative that's more open about its methods. Supporting apps and products that put effort into explaining their actions is one way to nudge the tech world toward better habits.

When you bump into issues like a chatbot that keeps misunderstanding specific names, or an app that feels unfair, don't assume it's just your problem. Companies depend on feedback from real people to fix blind spots. Most websites and apps have feedback forms or help emails.

**Here's an easy template you can use:**

> **Hi** [**Name**],
> **I noticed that** [describe the issue—be specific, like "the chatbot didn't recognize my name" or "the tool keeps recommending irrelevant items"]. **I think this might be affecting other users too. Is there a way to improve this? Thanks for listening!**
> **Best,**
> [**Your Name**]

You don't have to write an essay. Just point out what happened and why it matters. If you're using AI at work and see something off, flag it to IT or HR with a quick note. These messages help teams spot patterns and push for updates that benefit everyone.

Small choices add up. Turn on transparency features whenever they're available—these might show you what data an app collects or let you review past decisions made by the AI. If you spot a company promoting fairness audits or bias reviews, consider supporting their products over those that stay silent about these issues. Every click, every review, every conversation makes a difference.

Remember, your actions matter more than any technical knowledge. By staying alert, asking for clarity, and teaching others what you've discovered, you become part of the solution.

***Everyday Ethics Checklist***

- Pause before sharing AI-generated content; check accuracy and source.
- Choose tools that explain their results and data practices.
- Turn on transparency and privacy settings whenever possible.
- Give feedback about issues or unfair results; use simple, direct language.
- Support products from companies that address bias and fairness openly.
- Encourage respectful conversations about AI—even when there are no easy answers.

# CHAPTER 7
# STAYING CURRENT
YOUR AI JOURNEY BEYOND THIS BOOK

## 7.1 THE HOTTEST TRENDS—CHATGPT, GENERATIVE AI, AND WHAT'S NEXT

AI has quickly shifted from sci-fi dream to everyday tool, especially with the rise of ChatGPT and generative AI. People casually swap stories about getting help or inspiration from these tools, and AI-generated art is all over the internet. This is no longer a glimpse of the future—it's reshaping how we create, communicate, and solve problems right now.

Unlike old virtual assistants stuck on scripts, ChatGPT is powered by large language models trained on vast amounts of text. This allows it to generate responses that are strikingly human, whether you need writing suggestions, answers, or help with awkward emails. Instead of spitting out robotic replies, it can understand context, follow conversations, and respond with nuance. While it makes mistakes and can confidently present wrong info, it's a significant leap from the limited bots of the past.

Generative AI goes beyond text. Now you can describe a scene like "a dog wearing sunglasses on a beach at sunset" and get an instant, unique image. People without art backgrounds can now produce illustrations, posters, or logos in minutes. Some tools generate videos from scripts or transform rough sketches into polished designs. The same technologies are used for music, generating tunes from prompts, and even for cooking, by creating recipes from available ingredients. Education has also been transformed—generative AI builds personalized quizzes, adapts lesson plans, and simplifies textbook chapters for easier understanding.

Industries are rapidly adopting these advances. Marketers and small business owners use AI design tools to quickly create ads and social content. Musicians experiment with AI for melody ideas or audio touch-ups. Chefs invent recipes with AI's help. Teachers draft customized lessons using text generators that suit each student's needs. Customer support benefits from chatbots that can assess tone, respond to detailed queries, and escalate issues intelligently.

Looking forward, several key trends are emerging. One is "explainable AI," which aims to clarify how algorithms make decisions (such as approving loans or curating news) by providing easy-to-understand justifications. Synthetic data is giving AI new material to learn from without tapping into real, private data. Another key focus is responsible AI governance. Governments and organizations are creating rules to promote fairness, safety, and transparency. These efforts include new regulations, regular audits, and dedicated AI ethics teams that work to prevent unintended harm.

With the overwhelming hype, distinguishing real progress from buzzword-laden demos is crucial. Here's a handy checklist:

**Checklist: Separating Real Innovation from Hype**

- Is the tool in real use outside of tech circles, or just in demos?
- Does it have practical applications in daily life, or is it mainly for show?
- Does it raise privacy, fairness, or transparency concerns—are these being addressed?
- Is it integrated into familiar products, or does it require starting from scratch?
- Are there genuine examples of impact, not just promises?
- Are reputable organizations talking about or adopting it?
- Does it explain data usage? Can you control your data?

Staying current isn't about knowing every tool or trend, it's noticing what really sticks and how AI fits your needs or solves real problems. Whether your interest is creative, practical, or ethical, being mindful of these trends will give you a head start as AI continues to evolve.

## 7.2 AI NEWS—WHERE TO FIND RELIABLE UPDATES

Keeping up with AI often feels overwhelming, with new apps, jargon, and big claims appearing everywhere. Instead of trying to track every headline, focus on building a news routine that feeds your curiosity but stays manageable. For most people, subscribing to just two or three trusted AI newsletters or blogs is plenty. This helps you notice patterns over time and prevents information overload.

Choose publications that welcome beginners and break concepts down clearly. "The Algorithm" from MIT Technology Review is great for newcomers, offering practical updates, interviews, and straightforward explainers weekly—no technical background needed. Another good pick is Andrew Ng's "The Batch," which gives concise takes on breakthroughs, policy, and some AI mishaps, providing a broad picture without heavy jargon. For a broader context, BBC or Wired often focus on how AI impacts real people, not just the tech world, with accessible explainers on issues like self-driving cars and data privacy.

When choosing sources look for these three things:

- Credibility (does the author have experience in the field?)
- Transparency (are sources cited?)
- Freshness (is the material up-to-date?)

Ask:

- Are the writers named?
- Are there links to original research or announcements?
- Are articles current, or out-of-date?

If you can't easily answer these, it's better to look elsewhere.

Social media can be helpful if used carefully. Rather than following every trending account, select a handful of reliable sources like researchers, journalists, and educators on Twitter/X or LinkedIn who consistently break down trends without hype. If someone regularly shares reputable blogs or informative diagrams, they're worth following. Google Alerts are also effective. By setting up alerts for specific AI topics, you can receive targeted email summaries, keeping you up-to-date on what matters to you.

If you prefer a single dashboard, aggregator tools like Feedly can collect articles from various blogs and news outlets so you can quickly scan headlines and dive deeper only when interested. Flipboard offers a more visual experience, letting you flip through custom magazines for your preferred AI subjects. Both allow you to save articles for later, so you can binge-read when you have time and ignore the rest during busy periods.

When a story grabs your attention, resist the urge to share it immediately. Be sure to check the author's background. Are they credible or just repeating hearsay? Look for links to original data. If something seems too good or alarming to be true, check other reliable publications or search for fact-checks first.

This approach will gradually deepen your understanding of AI. Instead of being overwhelmed by every new trend or buzzword, you'll start recognizing which headlines signal genuine change and which are fleeting. You'll get comfortable saying, "I don't know yet—let me look it up," rather than feeling pressured to react to everything instantly.

By combining a few trusted newsletters, a social media feed you enjoy, and a simple news app, you can create an easy way to stay informed. It helps you keep up with the topics that matter most to you, at your own pace, without letting the news take over your day.

## 7.3 CURATED RESOURCES—BEST PODCASTS, COURSES, AND WEBSITES FOR BEGINNERS

If you're someone who likes to pick up new things while walking the dog or riding the bus, podcasts can be a great resource. "AI for Humans" is for anyone who doesn't want a heavy lecture. The hosts talk about new tools and stories in plain language, sometimes with humor, and often bring in real examples of how AI pops up in daily life. Another good option is "The AI Daily Brief." It gives short, sharp summaries of news and tech trends, letting you stay current with minimal effort. You don't have to listen every day—try one episode a week while you fold laundry or run errands. Podcasts are a great way to learn without even trying, and after a few weeks, you may notice yourself picking up new terms and ideas naturally.

Some people learn best by watching. YouTube is packed with explainers, but certain channels really stand out for making things visual and simple. "Two Minute Papers" takes research and turns it into bite-sized, animated overviews that are fun to watch. Think of it as show-and-tell for grownups who want to understand breakthroughs without feeling lost. "Crash Course AI" walks you through big concepts with illustrations, stories, and simple metaphors. If you're a fan of seeing diagrams drawn out as someone explains, these videos can make even tricky ideas stick.

A lot of folks worry that online courses will throw them into deep water with math or coding right away, but that's not always true. The "Elements of AI" course from the University of Helsinki is free, welcoming, and designed specifically for people with zero technical background. It mixes short readings, practical exercises, and quizzes so you can go at your own speed. Many learners say it feels more like chatting with a knowledgeable friend than surviving a lecture. LinkedIn Learning also offers several AI basics courses that start from scratch. These are video-based and broken into small chunks that let you track your progress. The platform occasionally requires a subscription, but many libraries and workplaces offer free access.

If you prefer learning by asking questions there are some forums that create a safe space. Artificial Intelligence Stack Exchange is a Q&A site where people of all backgrounds ask everything from "What is machine learning?" to "How do I know if my smart speaker is listening to me?" Moderators keep things supportive and discussions focused. Reddit's r/learnmachinelearning is another friendly zone that is famous for its "no stupid questions" threads. You can read through common beginner uncertainties or drop your own question without fear of judgment. Many people start by reading old threads for a month or two, then gradually join in once they see how open and welcoming the community can be.

To keep motivation high, consider setting small goals. You can listen to one podcast episode each week or watch one explainer video every Saturday morning. Maybe pick a course module to complete by the end of the month or set a reminder to check a forum thread every Friday evening.

Mixing different formats helps too. Some days you may want to listen and other days you may want to watch or read. Switching between podcasts, videos, articles, and forums keeps things fresh and prevents burnout. Try writing down three things that surprise you each week—whether it's a new term or an unexpected use case for AI—and see how your understanding grows over time.

Above all, remember that nobody expects perfection. Some resources will click with you, others won't and that's fine. Give yourself permission to sample widely until something sticks. If a course or channel feels too dry or complicated, skip it and move on. There's no single "right way" to learn about AI; what matters most is finding resources that fit your life and make you curious enough to keep going.

## 7.4 SETTING UP YOUR PERSONALIZED AI LEARNING PLAN

**To design your own AI learning plan:**

1. **Clarify your "why."**
   a. Decide why you want to learn AI:
      i. career growth
      ii. building new skills
      iii. curiosity
      iv. keeping up with kids
      v. running your business more efficiently
   b. Write down one or two reasons. This will keep you motivated when learning feels challenging or distractions get in the way.
2. **Set concrete goals.**
   a. Examples of clear goals:
      i. Learn to use a new AI app at work
      ii. Understand what AI bias is
      iii. Be able to explain what an algorithm does
   b. Specific goals make it easier to choose the right learning materials and track your progress.
3. **Choose your learning resources and schedule time.**
   a. Pick resources that match your goals, such as online courses, short articles, podcasts, or videos.
   b. Block out regular study time, even if it is just 15 minutes a day, to build steady progress.
   c. Keep it flexible—adjust the plan if a resource is too advanced or not engaging.

There's no right or wrong way to structure your learning plan. Consistency is key, not pace or session length. Some people learn best in groups, while others prefer to learn by themselves. If you're social, join an online study circle or invite a friend along. For added structure, try finding a mentor—someone just a step ahead, like a tech-savvy relative or coworker—and check in with them each month.

Tracking progress boosts motivation and helps learning stick. After reading an article, watching a video, or trying an AI tool, jot down what you did and how it felt. These notes mark milestones that build your confidence.

---

***Interactive Element: Building Your AI Learning Journal***

To track your AI learning journey, create a simple system you can stick with week after week. It can be as basic as a notebook or as organized as a spreadsheet—whatever you'll actually use.

- **Start with a title:** like "**My AI Learning Plan**" at the top of the first page.
- **Set your main goal:** Put it in big, clear letters so it stays front and center.
- **Create two columns:**
    - *What I Did*
    - *How It Went*
- **Fill in a new row each week:** Examples might include:
    - Watched a video on AI bias

    - Tried a chatbot
    - Explained data privacy to a neighbor
- **Record your reaction in the second column:** Note whether you felt confident, confused, excited, or frustrated.
- **Look for patterns over time:** You might discover that short videos work best for you, or that you thrive in discussions.

Try not to allow your plan to remain fixed. Every few months, pause and review. Ask yourself if your interests have shifted, if new AI trends intrigue you, or if work projects sparked new questions. Update your plan as needed. Swap out old resources and add new ones to keep things fresh. These regular reviews keep learning relevant and interesting.

If you lose momentum (which happens to everyone), don't stress. Life gets busy; plans can stall. The benefit of setting your own pace is that you can always pick up where you left off. Sometimes a break brings new insight when you return. If motivation is low, review your learning journal to see how much you've actually accomplished—progress is often more than it seems.

---

Above all, give yourself permission to experiment and adapt. No two learning plans are the same, because everyone's life is different. The best plan is the one that keeps you curious, engaged, and comfortable asking questions. Stay flexible, and you'll always find value in your efforts—even if your path changes along the way.

## 7.5 VISUAL GLOSSARY FOR QUICK REFERENCE

A clear, visual glossary cuts through confusion like nothing else. Imagine a reference guide you can hang on your wall, keep at your desk, or snap a photo of for your phone's lock screen. This isn't just a list of terms—it's a visual map of AI basics, organized for quick recall and daily reference.

Beyond single words, your guide could include at-a-glance visuals for common concepts. A neural network diagram, for example, uses dots and lines to show how information moves from input through layers to output. The point isn't memorizing every detail, but understanding how data moves through connected steps to reach answers.

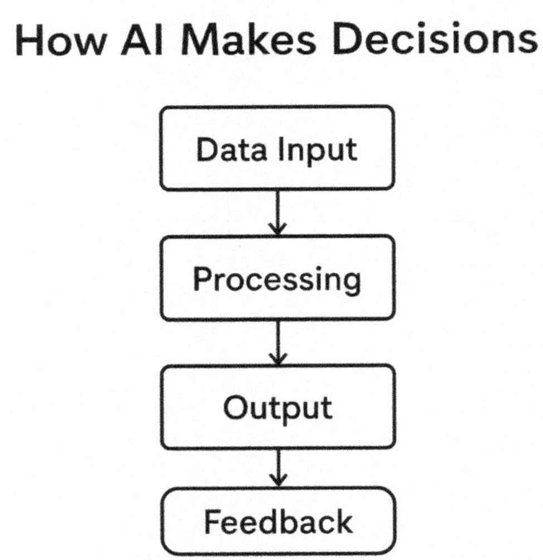

A flowchart illustrates "How AI Makes Decisions"—starting with data input, processing, and yielding output, sometimes followed by feedback.

Visuals like these help demystify what's happening inside AI tools such as smart assistants or recommendation systems. Customizing your glossary helps hands-on learners. Draw your own doodles. Stickers or colored pens add flair and make key ideas pop.

In the end, this reference tool helps make AI feel more approachable. Whether adjusting to changes at work or simply remembering what "inference" means while hearing it in the news, your visual glossary serves as a handy reference. Keep it within reach and update it as you go. Each time you see and apply these ideas in everyday life, your understanding grows stronger.

## 7.6 AI FOR LIFE—APPLYING WHAT YOU'VE LEARNED TO EVERYDAY DECISIONS

Every day, our choices, big and small, are influenced by technology. Now that you understand AI better, you can more easily identify what's genuinely useful, what's overhyped, and what deserves caution. Use this knowledge as a filter when deciding on gadgets, apps, or digital services. For instance, before installing a new smart home device or health tracker, ask: "What data is collected? Who can access it? Can I manage what's shared?" If an app requests unnecessary access to your contacts or microphone, you can confidently refuse or explore privacy settings, avoiding blanket acceptance of permissions.

Privacy isn't the only concern. You may notice odd patterns in AI-powered tools like recurring music recommendations, forms rejecting certain names, and apps failing to recognize a friend's face. These moments should trigger your awareness of possible bias. If you encounter biased outcomes, like a chatbot mishandling non-English names or facial recognition missing certain users, provide feedback or report the issue. Your input matters, as companies are starting to value user feedback that highlights these blind spots. In group settings at work or school, you can bring up whether a tool has been tested fairly across different users or if there's a way to challenge its decisions.

Ethical considerations go beyond surface-level questions. Thinking about facial recognition for home security, for example, raises important questions: Who else accesses the images? What if it misidentifies someone, like a neighbor? Create a simple decision tree: list benefits (convenience, security) against drawbacks (privacy risks, errors). If the downsides are significant or data use is unclear, you might seek a different system with better controls.

Health apps are another common place to apply your AI literacy. Before using a new health tracker, check if it allows reviewing, deleting, or exporting your data. Ask yourself if it genuinely helps your health understanding or merely adds unnecessary complexity. Always remember, no app or algorithm should substitute for a real doctor's advice—double-check suggestions with professionals.

As your confidence with AI grows, people may come to you with their questions. You might explain why an ad feels too targeted, or why a chatbot makes a particular mistake. These moments are ideal for sharing your knowledge, clarifying misconceptions, or walking someone through privacy settings. You don't need to be an expert. Being willing to talk about pros and cons helps others feel less intimidated.

Most importantly, stay curious. You don't need to know everything—AI develops quickly, and nobody is ever fully caught up. If you're confused or something seems off, keep investigating until you're comfortable. Treat every confusing app menu or unexpected result as a prompt to learn, not a setback. When tools update, experiment with new features. See if they add value or create new privacy or fairness questions.

Adaptability is crucial as AI changes. Some apps will disappear, and new ones will take their place with new promises and pitfalls. The key is to combine skepticism with curiosity. Be willing to admit, "I don't understand," but ready to explore until you do. This attitude will serve you with any emerging technology.

Wise AI use is about asking questions, identifying bias, making informed decisions, and helping others feel empowered. Curiosity and adaptability will keep you grounded through rapid change. Remember: AI doesn't need to be intimidating—it can enrich life if we use it thoughtfully and continue learning.

# CONCLUSION

The mission in writing this book was simple: empower readers. The goal was to build confidence with AI, at home, at work, and everywhere in between, without overwhelming anyone with jargon or making it seem like a computer science degree was required. AI is not a distant, untouchable concept. It is already present, influencing playlists, shaping email experiences, guiding shopping suggestions, and powering the helpful chatbot at the bank.

Let's take a quick look back through the steps we took together. We started by peeling away the mystery of AI. We tossed out the sci-fi robots and focused on the everyday reality—what AI is and what it isn't. You learned how to spot AI in today's world, whether it's sorting your photos, filtering spam, or helping you find the quickest route home. We dug into how AI "thinks", with recipes and city maps, not math formulas, so you could understand what's happening under the hood in plain English. You rolled up your sleeves and tried hands-on activities, from chatbots and smart speakers to image generators and AI art, discovering just how accessible these tools can be.

You learned how to make AI work for you at your job with things like automating tedious tasks, running smarter meetings, and decluttering your inbox. We explored how to spot bias, protect your privacy, and push for fairness in a world where not everything is transparent or equal. We busted myths at every turn, and we talked honestly about frustration, perfectionism, and the feeling that you're somehow behind. Most importantly, you built a toolkit for lifelong learning that includes cheatsheets, visual guides, and a handpicked resource list to keep you growing.

You know now that AI isn't magic or menace. You can confidently point out where it shows up in your day-to-day life—and you have the skills to start using it, not just watching from the sidelines. You've seen that you don't need to code or solve equations to understand how AI learns or to use its features. You've tried activities that let you experience the strengths and quirks of AI firsthand, in a safe and playful way. You know how to use AI tools to save time, collaborate, and make your work life a little less chaotic. You can spot and name bias, ask thoughtful questions about privacy, and check the hype when you see splashy headlines. You're no longer a beginner. You're a participant.

But here's the real heart of it: none of this matters if it just sits on the page. We encourage you to pick one thing from this book and try it. Maybe it's asking your smart speaker a new question. Maybe it's using an AI-powered meeting tool at work, or creating a mind map of AI terms to share at your next family dinner. Revisit your personal AI cheatsheet. Pick a resource from the curated list, add it to your bookmarks, and share what you've learned. Whether it's with a friend, a coworker, or a curious kid, one of the best ways to learn is to teach or explain something new. You'll be amazed at how much deeper your understanding gets when you put it into words for someone else.

AI isn't going to freeze in place just because you finished this book. Things will keep moving. New apps will appear. Old ones will change. Some features will break, new ones will surprise you and that's okay. Critical thinking and resourcefulness will keep you steady, no matter how the tech landscape shifts.

Please don't let this be the last time you flip through these pages. Bookmark the visual glossary. Keep your cheatsheet handy—tape it to your fridge, pin it to your desktop, or keep a photo on your phone. These aren't just study aids; they're your compass. And when you want to keep learning, come back to the resources list. Try a new podcast or video explainer, or join a friendly online forum. If you ever feel lost in the noise, remember: you know exactly where to look for clear, honest answers.

Use what you've learned. Ask the next question. When someone around you says, "AI is too complicated," show them your cheatsheet, or explain something you've discovered. Don't worry about being the expert. Stay curious, stay open, and take pride in being someone willing to learn, adapt, and help others do the same. You're not just using AI now—you're shaping how it fits into your life.

## KEEPING THE GAME ALIVE

Now you have what you need to start using AI with confidence. The best way to keep this knowledge alive is to share it with others.

Your review can guide the next beginner who feels unsure where to start. A few quick words about what helped you most could make all the difference.

Leaving a review takes less than a minute, costs nothing, and could help another learner take their first step into AI.

👉 Scan the QR code below to leave your review:

Thank you for being part of this journey. Together, we can make AI easier and more approachable for everyone.

– **Atwater Publishing**

# REFERENCES


Carlson School of Management. (n.d.). *Debunking 5 artificial intelligence myths*. University of Minnesota. Retrieved from https://carlsonschool.umn.edu/graduate/resources/debunking-5-artificial-intelligence-myths

Constitutional Discourse. (n.d.). *Making the invisible visible: Explainable AI in everyday life*. Retrieved from https://constitutionaldiscourse.com/making-the-invisible-visible-explainable-ai-in-everyday-life-part-i/

Coursera. (n.d.). *What are AI algorithms?* Retrieved from https://www.coursera.org/articles/ai-algorithms

Ferrara, E. (2023). *Fairness and bias in artificial intelligence: A brief survey of sources, impacts, and mitigation strategies. arXiv Preprint*. https://arxiv.org/abs/2304.07683

Freedom Forum. (n.d.). *How to spot a deepfake: Tips, tools and more*. Retrieved from https://www.freedomforum.org/how-to-spot-a-deepfake/

GearBrain. (n.d.). *AI in smart homes: Security, efficiency & automation*. Retrieved from https://www.gearbrain.com/ai-smart-home-automation-devices-2671168897.html

Good Things Foundation Australia. (2024, September). *How to use Otter.ai*. Good Things Foundation Australia. Retrieved August 12, 2025, from https://goodthingsaustralia.org/mentor-resource/how-to-use-otter-ai/

Google. (n.d.). *AI tools for business*. Retrieved from https://workspace.google.com/solutions/ai/

Heinz College, Carnegie Mellon University. (2023, July). *Artificial intelligence, explained*. Retrieved from https://www.heinz.cmu.edu/media/2023/July/artificial-intelligence-explained

IBM. (2023, December 22). *What is AI bias?* Retrieved from https://www.ibm.com/think/topics/ai-bias

IBM Community. (2025, March 21). *ABCs of AI: Visual glossary for entry-level AI education*. Retrieved from https://community.ibm.com/community/user/ai-datascience/blogs/thalia-barry/2025/03/21/abcs-of-ai-visual-glossary-for-entry-level-ai-educ

Indeed. (n.d.). *What is AI resume screening? A guide for employers*. Retrieved from https://www.indeed.com/hire/c/info/ai-resume-screening

Litslink. (n.d.). *How does Netflix use AI to personalize recommendations?* Retrieved from https://litslink.com/blog/all-about-netflix-artificial-intelligence-the-truth-behind-personalized-content

MDPI. (2023). *Analysing urban traffic patterns with neural networks and deep learning. Applied Sciences, 14*(17), 7793. https://www.mdpi.com/2076-3417/14/17/7793

MDPI. (2021). *Fairness and bias in artificial intelligence: A brief survey of sources, impacts, and mitigation strategies. Philosophies, 6*(1), 3. https://www.mdpi.com/2413-4155/6/1/3

Moluguri, V. K. (n.d.). *Google's Teachable Machine AI: Step-by-step tutorial included*. Medium. Retrieved from https://vinaykumarmoluguri.medium.com/googles-teachable-machine-ai-step-by-step-tutorial-included-6a7200199932

NoCodeExits. (n.d.). *10+ real stories of no-code AI*. Retrieved from https://www.nocodeexits.com/no-code-ai

Planorama Design. (n.d.). *Avoiding information overload from AI*. Retrieved from https://planorama.design/blog/avoiding-information-overload-from-ai/

PopSci. (n.d.). *How to create routines for Alexa, Siri, and Google Assistant*. Retrieved from https://www.popsci.com/routines-for-digital-assistants/

Reddit. (2024). *Which tools have you found most effective for visual learning? r/edtech*. Retrieved from https://www.reddit.com/r/edtech/comments/1go5xda/which_tools_have_you_found_most_effective_for/

StrataScratch. (n.d.). *Data science vs. machine learning vs. deep learning: The difference*. Retrieved from https://www.stratascratch.com/blog/data-science-vs-machine-learning-vs-deep-learning-the-difference/

Techie Gist. (n.d.). *A playful cooking analogy to demystify AI models*. Retrieved from https://techiegist.hashnode.dev/cooking-up-ai-models-a-flavorful-journey-through-data-and-algorithms

Technology Review. (2024, September 13). *Conspiracy-debunking chatbots, and fact-checking AI*. MIT Technology Review. Retrieved from https://www.technologyreview.com/2024/09/13/1103952/the-download-conspiracy-debunking-chatbots-and-fact-checking-ai/

UX Magazine. (n.d.). *I tested 7 free AI image generators. This one's my pick*. Retrieved from https://uxmag.com/articles/i-tested-7-free-ai-image-generators-this-ones-my-pick

Vinaykumarmoluguri. (n.d.). *Google Bard vs. ChatGPT: Step-by-step guide*. Vocal Media Journal. Retrieved from https://vocal.media/journal/google-bard-vs-chat-gpt-step-by-step-guide